ClearRevise®

Edexcel GCSE
Physical Education 1PE0

Illustrated revision and practice

Published by
PG Online Limited
The Old Coach House
35 Main Road
Tolpuddle
Dorset
DT2 7EW
United Kingdom

sales@pgonline.co.uk
www.clearrevise.com
www.pgonline.co.uk
2023

PREFACE

Absolute clarity! That's the aim.

This is everything you need to ace the exams and beam with pride. Each topic is laid out in a beautifully illustrated format that is clear, approachable and as concise and simple as possible.

Each section of the specification is clearly indicated to help you cross-reference your revision. The checklist on the contents pages will help you keep track of what you have already worked through and what's left before the big day.

We have included worked exam-style questions with answers. There is also a set of exam-style questions at the end of each section for you to practise writing answers. You can check your answers against those given at the end of the book.

LEVELS OF LEARNING

Based on the degree to which you are able to truly understand a new topic, we recommend that you work in stages. Start by reading a short explanation of something, then try to recall what you've just read. This will have a limited effect if you stop there but it aids the next stage. Question everything. Write down your own summary and then complete and mark a related exam-style question. Cover up the answers if necessary but learn from them once you've seen them. Lastly, teach someone else. Explain the topic in a way that they can understand. Have a go at the different practice questions – they offer an insight into how and where marks are awarded.

ACKNOWLEDGEMENTS

The questions in this ClearRevise guide are the sole responsibility of the authors and have neither been provided nor approved by the examination board.

Every effort has been made to trace and acknowledge ownership of copyright. The publishers will be happy to make any future amendments with copyright owners that it has not been possible to contact. The publisher would like to thank the following companies and individuals who granted permission for the use of their images and extracts in this textbook.

Longjumper © Stefan Holm / SHUTTERSTOCK.com
Cricket bowler © 2007 Eric Gevaert/Shutterstock.
Pommel horse routine © Michele Morrone / Shutterstock.com
Longjumper 2013 © Pavel L Photo and Video/Shutterstock.
Throw-in © katatonia82 / SHUTTERSTOCK.com
Header in Juventus game © 2021 Ettore Griffoni/Shutterstock.
Long jump take-off © John Bingham / Alamy Stock Photo
Kayak sprint © Celso Pupo / SHUTTERSTOCK.com
England rugby union conversion kick © 2019 atsportphoto/Shutterstock.com
Rugby 7s match © Mai Groves / SHUTTERSTOCK.com
Cross country jump © Anthony Delgado / SHUTTERSTOCK.com
London Marathon © IR Stone / SHUTTERSTOCK.com
Boxing match © Dmitry Niko / SHUTTERSTOCK.com
Rugby union head injury © Ettore Griffoni / Shutterstock.
Discus thrower © Shahjehan / SHUTTERSTOCK.com
Road cyclists © Paul Higley / SHUTTERSTOCK.com
World Boxing Championships match © Paolo Bona / Shutterstock.com

Marissa Papaconstantinou © Avpics / Alamy Stock Photo
Chris Froome © Radu Razvan / SHUTTERSTOCK.com
Nafissatou Thiam © SPP Sport Press Photo. / Alamy Stock Photo
AJ MacGinty © Action Plus Sports Images / Alamy Stock Photo
Rachel Daly © Jose Breton- Pics Action / SHUTTERSTOCK.com
Pattaya Tadtong © FocusDzign / SHUTTERSTOCK.com
Camera operator © Paolo Bona / SHUTTERSTOCK.com
Sponsorship boards © Jordan Tan / SHUTTERSTOCK.com
England Women's Rugby Team © atsportphoto / SHUTTERSTOCK.com
Rolex store © Dr. Victor Wong / SHUTTERSTOCK.com
Rory McIlroy © Gary Yee / SHUTTERSTOCK.com
England Women's Football © Influential Photography / SHUTTERSTOCK.com
Taylor / da Silva tackle © PA Images / Alamy Stock Photo
Juventus Shirt © charnsitr / SHUTTERSTOCK.com
David Warner © News Images LTD / Alamy Stock Photo
Tonya Harding © PA Images / Alamy Stock Photo

Design and artwork: Jessica Webb / PG Online Ltd
First edition 2023   10 9 8 7 6 5 4 3 2 1
A catalogue entry for this book is available from the British Library
ISBN: 978-1-916518-05-6
With contributions from R Howitt
Copyright © PG Online 2023
All rights reserved
No part of this publication may be reproduced, stored in a retrieval system, or transmitted in any form or by any means without the prior written permission of the copyright owner.

Printed on FSC® certified paper by Bell and Bain Ltd, Glasgow, UK.

THE SCIENCE OF REVISION

Illustrations and words

Research has shown that revising with words and pictures doubles the quality of responses by students.[1] This is known as 'dual-coding' because it provides two ways of fetching the information from our brain. The improvement in responses is particularly apparent in students when they are asked to apply their knowledge to different problems. Recall, application and judgement are all specifically and carefully assessed in public examination questions.

Retrieval of information

Retrieval practice encourages students to come up with answers to questions.[2] The closer the question is to one you might see in a real examination, the better. Also, the closer the environment in which a student revises is to the 'examination environment', the better. Students who had a test 2–7 days away did 30% better using retrieval practice than students who simply read, or repeatedly reread material. Students who were expected to teach the content to someone else after their revision period did better still.[3] What was found to be most interesting in other studies is that students using retrieval methods and testing for revision were also more resilient to the introduction of stress.[4]

Ebbinghaus' forgetting curve and spaced learning

Ebbinghaus' 140-year-old study examined the rate at which we forget things over time. The findings still hold true. However, the act of forgetting facts and techniques and relearning them is what cements them into the brain.[5] Spacing out revision is more effective than cramming – we know that, but students should also know that the space between revisiting material should vary depending on how far away the examination is. A cyclical approach is required. An examination 12 months away necessitates revisiting covered material about once a month. A test in 30 days should have topics revisited every 3 days – intervals of roughly a tenth of the time available.[6]

Summary

Students: the more tests and past questions you do, in an environment as close to examination conditions as possible, the better you are likely to perform on the day. If you prefer to listen to music while you revise, tunes without lyrics will be far less detrimental to your memory and retention. Silence is most effective.[5] If you choose to study with friends, choose carefully – effort is contagious.[7]

---

1. Mayer, R. E., & Anderson, R. B. (1991). Animations need narrations: An experimental test of dual-coding hypothesis. *Journal of Education Psychology*, (83)4, 484–490.
2. Roediger III, H. L., & Karpicke, J.D. (2006). Test-enhanced learning: Taking memory tests improves long-term retention. *Psychological Science*, 17(3), 249–255.
3. Nestojko, J., Bui, D., Kornell, N. & Bjork, E. (2014). Expecting to teach enhances learning and organisation of knowledge in free recall of text passages. *Memory and Cognition*, 42(7), 1038–1048.
4. Smith, A. M., Floerke, V. A., & Thomas, A. K. (2016) Retrieval practice protects memory against acute stress. *Science*, 354(6315), 1046–1048.
5. Perham, N., & Currie, H. (2014). Does listening to preferred music improve comprehension performance? *Applied Cognitive Psychology*, 28(2), 279–284.
6. Cepeda, N. J., Vul, E., Rohrer, D., Wixted, J. T. & Pashler, H. (2008). Spacing effects in learning a temporal ridgeline of optimal retention. *Psychological Science*, 19(11), 1095–1102.
7. Busch, B. & Watson, E. (2019), *The Science of Learning*, 1st ed. Routledge.

CONTENTS

Paper 1   Fitness and body systems
Topic 1   Applied anatomy and physiology

Specification point

1.1.1	The functions of the skeleton	2
1.1.2	Classification of bones	3
1.1.3	Skeletal structure	4
1.1.4	Classification of joints	6
1.1.5	Movement possibilities at joints	7
1.1.6	The role of ligaments and tendons	8
1.1.7	Classification and characteristics of muscle types	9
1.1.8	Location and role of the voluntary muscular system	10
1.1.9	Antagonistic pairs of muscles	11
1.1.10	Characteristics of fast and slow twitch muscle fibre types	12
1.1.11	How the skeletal and muscular systems work together	13
1.2.1	Functions of the cardiovascular system	14
1.2.2	Structure of the cardiovascular system	15
1.2.3, 1.2.4, 1.2.5	Blood vessels, blood flow and blood cells	16
1.2.6	Composition of inhaled and exhaled air	18
1.2.7	Vital capacity and tidal volume	19
1.2.8, 1.2.9	Structure and function of the respiratory system	20
1.2.10, 1.4.4	How the cardiovascular and respiratory systems work together	22
1.3.1, 1.3.2	Aerobic and anaerobic exercise	23
1.4.1, 1.4.2, 1.4.3	The short-term effects of exercise	24
1.4.6	Heart rate, stroke volume and cardiac output	26
	Examination practice: Topic 1	27

Topic 2   Movement analysis

Specification point

2.1.1	Lever systems	30
2.1.2	Mechanical advantage and disadvantage	32
2.2	Movement patterns using body planes and axes	33
	Examination practice: Topic 2	34

Topic 3   Physical training

Specification point

3.1	Health and fitness	35
3.2.1, 3.2.2	The components of fitness	36
3.2.2, 3.2.3, 3.2.4	Fitness tests	38

Spec	Topic	Page
3.2.5, 3.3.1	The principles of training	43 ☐
3.2.5, 3.3.1	Thresholds of training	44 ☐
3.2.5, 3.3.2, 3.3.3	Types of training	45 ☐
3.2.5, 3.3.2, 3.3.3	Fitness classes	50 ☐
3.4.1, 3.4.2, 3.4.3	The long-term effects of exercise on the muscular-skeletal system	51 ☐
3.4.1, 3.4.2, 3.4.4	The long-term effects of exercise on the cardio-respiratory system	52 ☐
3.5.1	PARQ assessments	54 ☐
3.5.2	Injury prevention	55 ☐
3.5.3	Injuries that can occur in physical activity and sport	56 ☐
3.5.4	RICE	57 ☐
3.5.5	Performance-enhancing drugs (PEDs)	58 ☐
3.5.5	Types of performers that may use different types of PEDs	60 ☐
3.6.1	The purpose and importance of warm-ups and cool downs	61 ☐
3.6.2, 3.6.3	Phases and activities of warm-ups and cool downs	62 ☐
	Examination practice: Topic 3	64 ☐

Paper 2 Health and performance

Topic 1 Health, fitness and well-being

Specification point ☑

Spec	Topic	Page
1.1.1	Physical health	68 ☐
1.1.2, 1.1.3, 1.1.4	Emotional and social health	69 ☐
1.1.5	How to promote personal health	70 ☐
1.1.6, 1.1.7	Lifestyle choices in diet, activity level and the work/rest/sleep balance	71 ☐
1.1.6, 1.1.7	Lifestyle choices in relation to legal recreational drugs	72 ☐
1.2	The consequences of a sedentary lifestyle	74 ☐
1.3.1	Balanced diet	76 ☐
1.3.2	The role and importance of macronutrients	77 ☐
1.3.3	The role and importance of micronutrients	78 ☐
1.3.3, 1.3.4, 1.3.6	The factors affecting optimum weight	79 ☐
1.3.7	Hydration for physical activity and sport	80 ☐
	Examination practice: Topic 1	81 ☐

Topic 2 Sport psychology

Specification point ☑

Spec	Topic	Page
2.1	Classification of skills	84 ☐
2.2	Goal setting with SMART targets	86 ☐
2.3.1, 2.3.2	Types of guidance	88 ☐
2.3.3, 2.3.4	Types of feedback to optimise performance	90 ☐
2.4	Mental preparation for performance	92 ☐
	Examination practice: Topic 2	93 ☐

Topic 3 Socio-cultural influences

Specification point

			☑
3.1	Engagement patterns of different social groups in physical activity and sport	95	☐
3.2.1	Commercialisation, the media and sport	99	☐
3.2.2, 3.2.3	Advantages and disadvantages of commercialisation and the media	100	☐
3.3.1, 3.3.2	Types of sporting behaviour	102	☐
	Examination practice: Topic 3	104	☐

Topic 4 The use of data

			☑
4.1.1, 4.1.2	Understanding how data is collected	108	☐
4.1.1, 4.1.3	Presenting data	109	☐
4.1.4, 4.1.5	Analysis and evaluation of data	110	☐
	Examination practice	112	☐

Non-exam assessment (NEA)

		☑
Practical performances	114	☐
Analysis and evaluation or performance	115	☐

Examination practice answers	**116**
Levels-based mark schemes for extended response questions	123
Command words	125
Index	126
Examination tips	**129**

MARK ALLOCATIONS

Green mark allocations[1] on answers to in-text questions throughout this guide help to indicate where marks are gained within the answers. A bracketed '1' e.g. [1] = one valid point worthy of a mark.

In longer answer questions, a mark is given based on the whole response. In these answers, a tick mark [✓] indicates that a valid point has been made. For a mark, a judgement should be made using the levels-based mark scheme on **page 123**.

There are often many more points to make than there are marks available so you have more opportunity to max out your answers than you may think.

TOPICS FOR PAPER 1
Fitness and body systems (1PE0/01)

Information about Component 1

Mandatory written exam: 1 hour 30 minutes
80 marks
36% of the qualification grade
Externally assessed.
All questions are mandatory.
Use black ink. You can use an HB pencil, but only for graphs and diagrams.
Calculators are permitted in this examination.

Specification coverage
Topic 1: Applied anatomy and physiology
Topic 2: Movement analysis
Topic 3: Physical training
Topic 4: Use of data (Page 108)

Questions
The assessment consists of multiple-choice, short-answer, long-answer and one extended writing question.
The use of data is embedded throughout the paper where appropriate.

1.1.1
THE FUNCTIONS OF THE SKELETON

The skeletal system provides a framework for movement. The muscular system attaches to the skeleton. When muscles contract, they pull the bones.

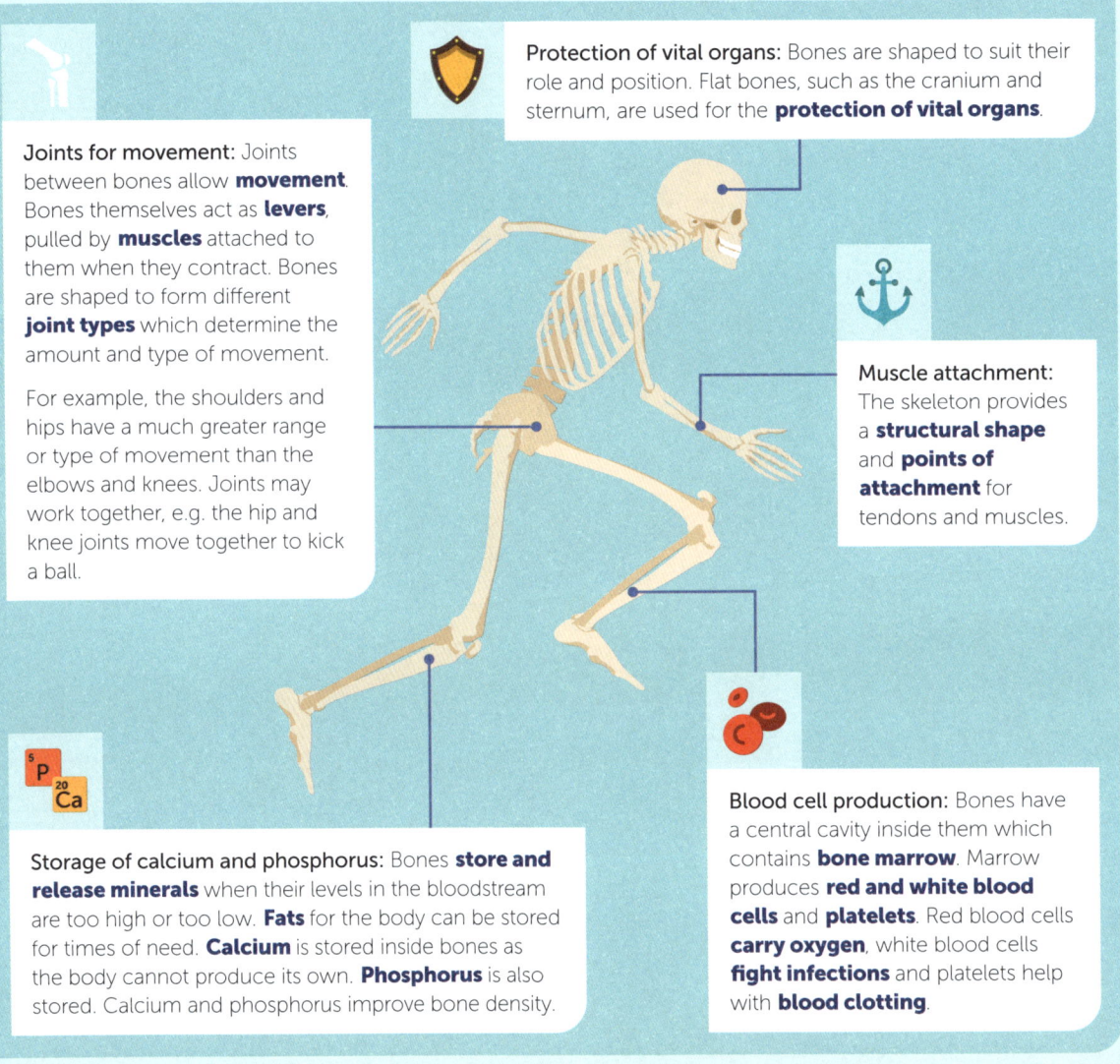

Protection of vital organs: Bones are shaped to suit their role and position. Flat bones, such as the cranium and sternum, are used for the **protection of vital organs**.

Joints for movement: Joints between bones allow **movement**. Bones themselves act as **levers**, pulled by **muscles** attached to them when they contract. Bones are shaped to form different **joint types** which determine the amount and type of movement.

For example, the shoulders and hips have a much greater range or type of movement than the elbows and knees. Joints may work together, e.g. the hip and knee joints move together to kick a ball.

Muscle attachment: The skeleton provides a **structural shape** and **points of attachment** for tendons and muscles.

Storage of calcium and phosphorus: Bones **store and release minerals** when their levels in the bloodstream are too high or too low. **Fats** for the body can be stored for times of need. **Calcium** is stored inside bones as the body cannot produce its own. **Phosphorus** is also stored. Calcium and phosphorus improve bone density.

Blood cell production: Bones have a central cavity inside them which contains **bone marrow**. Marrow produces **red and white blood cells** and **platelets**. Red blood cells **carry oxygen**, white blood cells **fight infections** and platelets help with **blood clotting**.

Maya plays rugby union.
    (a) State **one** way in which Maya's skeleton protects her vital organs during a game. [1]
    (b) Explain, with the use of a related sporting example, how Maya's bones allow movement. [2]

(a) Her ribs will protect her heart and lungs in a scrum or tackle.[1] Her skull helps to protect her brain in a tackle.[1] Her sternum will protect her chest in a tackle.[1]
(b) The femur acts as a lever[1] to generate speed when running to gain ground.[1] Muscles attached to bones pull the ulna/radius/femur to impart a force / range of motion on the ball when kicking / passing.[1] This allows Maya to pass more quickly / take longer penalties to benefit gameplay.[1]

1.1.2

CLASSIFICATION OF BONES

The shape and type of bones determine their role within the body.

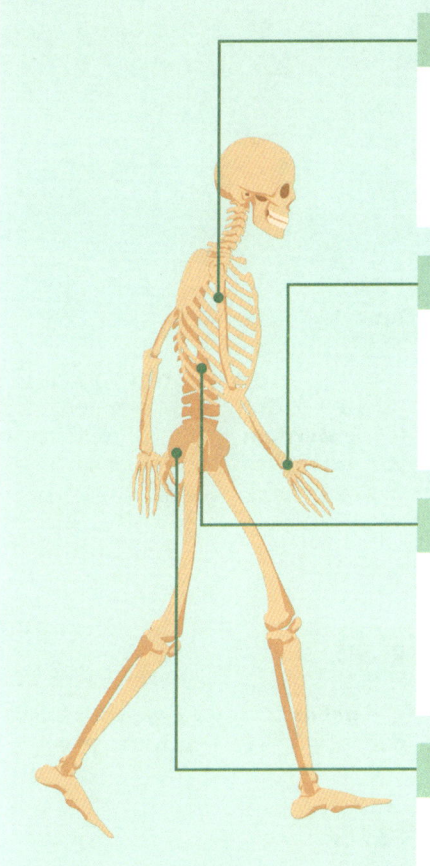

Long bones (leverage)

Long bones are longer than they are wide. They enable **gross movement**, for example the **femur** and **humerus**. They provide leverage for physical movement such as running, jumping and throwing.

Short bones (weight bearing)

Short bones are cube shaped, for example the **carpals** and **tarsals** (page 5) in the wrist and ankles. These spread loads and absorb shock. This is important in running as the foot strikes the ground or in cricket as the bat strikes a ball.

Flat bones (protection and muscle attachment)

Flat bones, such as the **sternum**, **ribs** and **cranium**, provide protection for vital organs and a broad surface area for muscle attachment. This aids performers in contact sports and for general movement.

Irregular bones (protection and muscle attachment)

Irregular bones, such the **vertebrae** and **pelvis**, have a complex shape and structure to perform their functions of protecting organs and the spinal cord. They also provide a strong attachment surface for muscles.

Complete the table below to state:
- (a) The classification of each bone and, [1]
- (b) The function for each classification. [2]

Bones	Classification	Function of the classification
Phalanges	(a)(i)	(b)(i)
Tarsals	(a)(ii)	(b)(ii)
Ribs	(a)(iii)	(b)(iii)

(a) (i) Long bones[1]   (ii) Short bones[1]   (iii) Flat bones.[1]
(b) (i) Leverage[1]   (ii) Load bearing[1]   (iii) Protection of organs[1] / Muscle attachment[1]

Edexcel GCSE Physical Education – Paper 1, Topic 1

SKELETAL STRUCTURE

The structure and function of the musculoskeletal system depends on the location of major bones and joints within the skeleton.

Bones in the human body

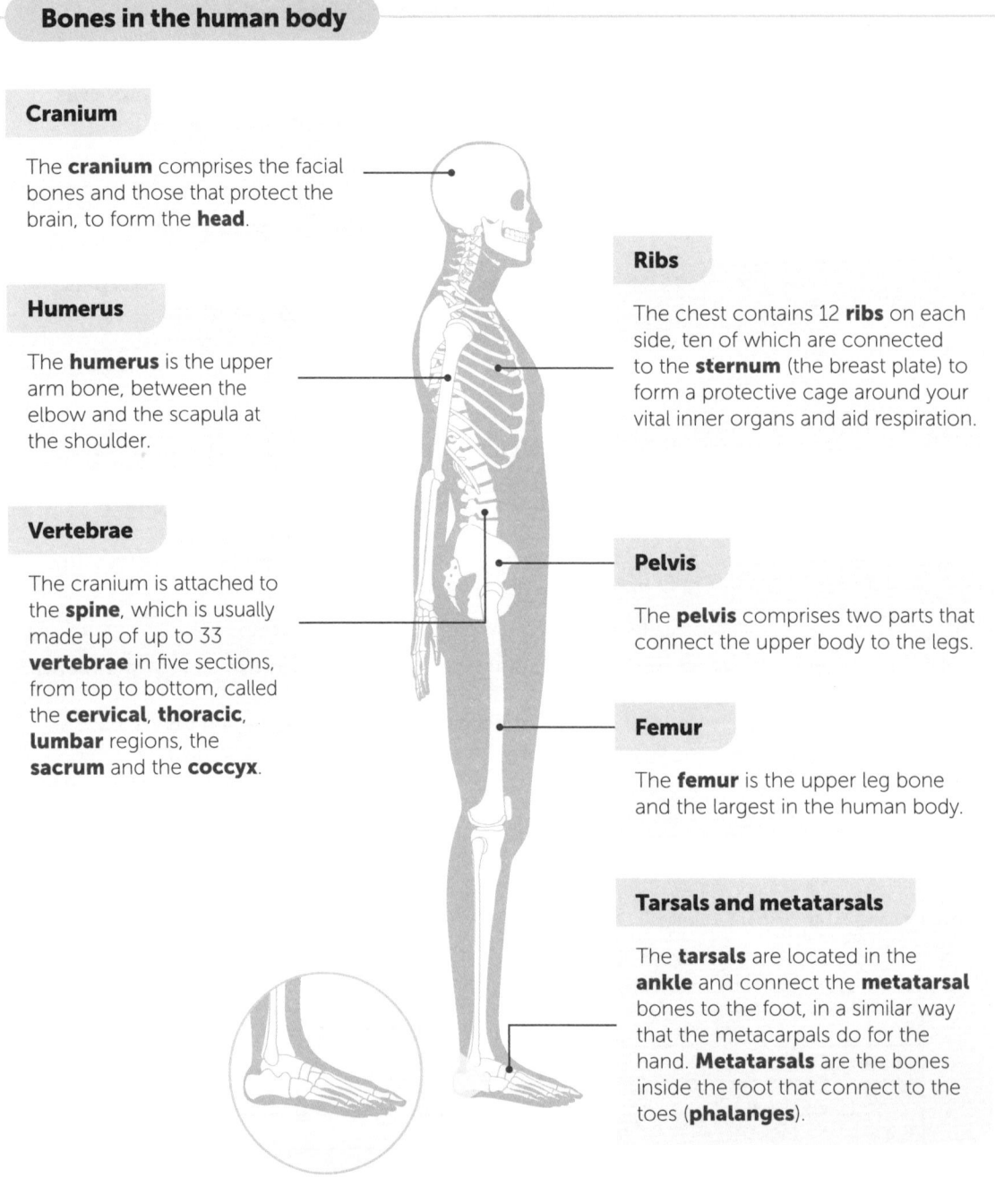

Cranium

The **cranium** comprises the facial bones and those that protect the brain, to form the **head**.

Humerus

The **humerus** is the upper arm bone, between the elbow and the scapula at the shoulder.

Vertebrae

The cranium is attached to the **spine**, which is usually made up of up to 33 **vertebrae** in five sections, from top to bottom, called the **cervical**, **thoracic**, **lumbar** regions, the **sacrum** and the **coccyx**.

Ribs

The chest contains 12 **ribs** on each side, ten of which are connected to the **sternum** (the breast plate) to form a protective cage around your vital inner organs and aid respiration.

Pelvis

The **pelvis** comprises two parts that connect the upper body to the legs.

Femur

The **femur** is the upper leg bone and the largest in the human body.

Tarsals and metatarsals

The **tarsals** are located in the **ankle** and connect the **metatarsal** bones to the foot, in a similar way that the metacarpals do for the hand. **Metatarsals** are the bones inside the foot that connect to the toes (**phalanges**).

> A downhill skier has fallen with a suspected fracture of the lower leg, above the ankle.
> Name **one** of the bones that they may have fractured. [1]
>
> Tibia,[1] or fibula.[1]

Infants are born with about 270 bones in their skeleton to provide extra flexibility. During childhood, many bones fuse together ending up with typically 210 bones in the adult skeleton.

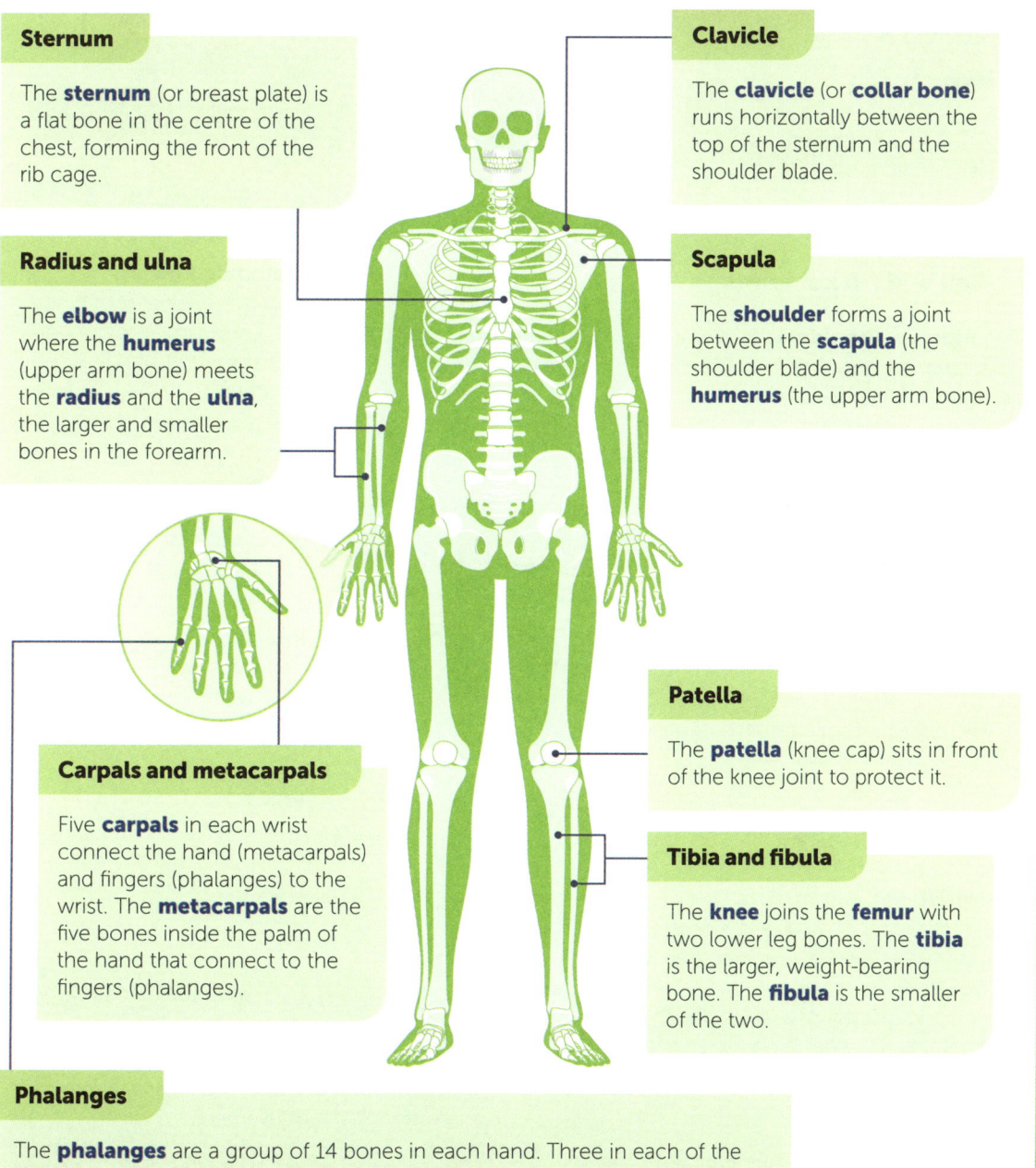

Sternum

The **sternum** (or breast plate) is a flat bone in the centre of the chest, forming the front of the rib cage.

Radius and ulna

The **elbow** is a joint where the **humerus** (upper arm bone) meets the **radius** and the **ulna**, the larger and smaller bones in the forearm.

Carpals and metacarpals

Five **carpals** in each wrist connect the hand (metacarpals) and fingers (phalanges) to the wrist. The **metacarpals** are the five bones inside the palm of the hand that connect to the fingers (phalanges).

Phalanges

The **phalanges** are a group of 14 bones in each hand. Three in each of the **fingers** and two in the thumb. They are also found in the **toes** of each foot.

Clavicle

The **clavicle** (or **collar bone**) runs horizontally between the top of the sternum and the shoulder blade.

Scapula

The **shoulder** forms a joint between the **scapula** (the shoulder blade) and the **humerus** (the upper arm bone).

Patella

The **patella** (knee cap) sits in front of the knee joint to protect it.

Tibia and fibula

The **knee** joins the **femur** with two lower leg bones. The **tibia** is the larger, weight-bearing bone. The **fibula** is the smaller of the two.

Edexcel GCSE **Physical Education – Paper 1, Topic 1**

1.1.4

CLASSIFICATION OF JOINTS

Different types or classifications of joint allow different ranges of movement.

Pivot joints

The **neck** is an example of a pivot joint. Pivot joints allow rotational movement in one plane (uniaxial).

Neck

Articulating vertebrae: atlas (C1) and axis (C2).

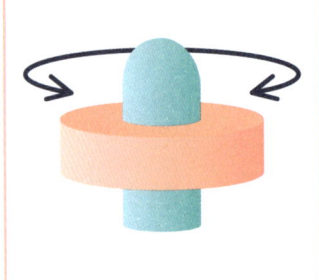

Ball and socket joints

The **hips** and **shoulders** are examples of ball and socket joints. A ball-shaped end of one bone fits into a cup-shaped socket in another. This allows for flexion and extension, abduction and adduction, circumduction and rotational movement in almost all directions, making sporting actions such as a cricket bowl or breaststroke swimming possible.

Hip

Articulating bones: pelvis, femur.

Shoulder

Articulating bones: humerus, scapula.

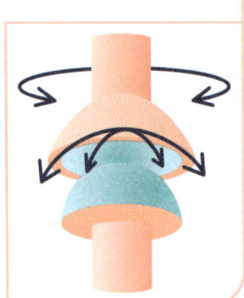

Condyloid joints

The **wrist** is an example of a condyloid joint. It is similar to a ball and socket joint but as the socket is ovular, it only allows movement in two planes (biaxially) with flexion and extension, and abduction and adduction. There is no rotation.

Wrist

Articulating bones: radius, carpals.

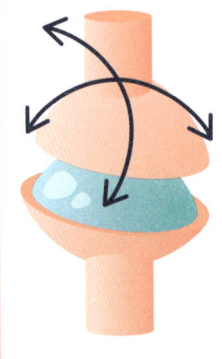

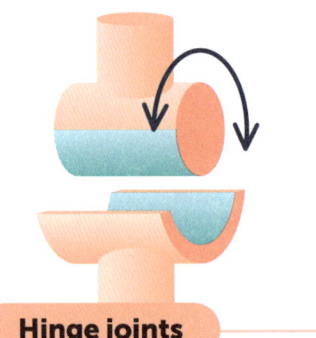

Hinge joints

The **elbows**, **knees** and **ankles** are examples of hinge joints. They allow movement in one plane through flexion and extension with up to 180 degrees of motion.

Elbow

Articulating bones: humerus, radius, ulna.

Knee

Articulating bones: femur, tibia.

Ankle

Articulating bones: talus, tibia, and fibula.

---

1. State **one** type of joint with a single plane of movement. [1]
2. State the type of joint that allows the greatest range of movement. [1]

1. Pivot / hinge joint.[1]
2. Ball and socket joint.[1]

MOVEMENT POSSIBILITIES AT JOINTS

The following types of movement are linked to specific types of joint, which enable that movement to take place.

Flexion and extension

Flexion and **extension** occurs at the hips and shoulders, and at hinge joints such as the **elbows** and **knees**, as the angle of the joint closes and opens.

Flexion in the upward phase of a bicep curl

Extension with a backhand shot in tennis

Plantar flexion and dorsiflexion

These are specialist terms for flexion and extension at the **ankle**. **Plantar flexion** means to point the toes. **Dorsiflexion** means to lift the end of the foot at the toes, pivoting at the heel.

Plantar flexion in ballet

Dorsiflexion in long jump

Abduction and adduction

Abduction and **adduction** at the shoulder means to take your arms away (to abduct) from the body, or bringing them back towards (to adduct) the midline of the body. A star jump uses both abduction and adduction.

Abduction in butterfly swimming

Adduction in pull-ups on the rings

Rotation and circumduction

Rotation of the shoulder creates a twisting of the bone along its long axis, such as when you rotate your palm up towards the sky.

Circumduction (think circumference) means a circular movement of a limb around the ball and socket joint.

The two movements are often combined.

Shoulder circumduction in bowling

Shoulder rotation on the pommel horse

Identify which joint type allows abduction and adduction. [1]

Ball and socket joint. [1]

Edexcel GCSE **Physical Education** – Paper 1, Topic 1

THE ROLE OF LIGAMENTS AND TENDONS

Ligaments and **tendons** are found in joints. Ligaments connect bone to bone. Tendons are used to connect bone to muscle.

Structure of the knee

The knee is an example of a **synovial joint** that contains several important ligaments and tendons designed to prevent injury.

Tendons are a tough yet flexible band of fibrous tissue which join **muscles to bones**, pulling them when muscles contract.

Ligaments are short bands of tough and elastic tissue **connecting bones together** and stabilising a joint to prevent dislocation or injury during exercise. Elasticity in the ligaments absorbs shock.

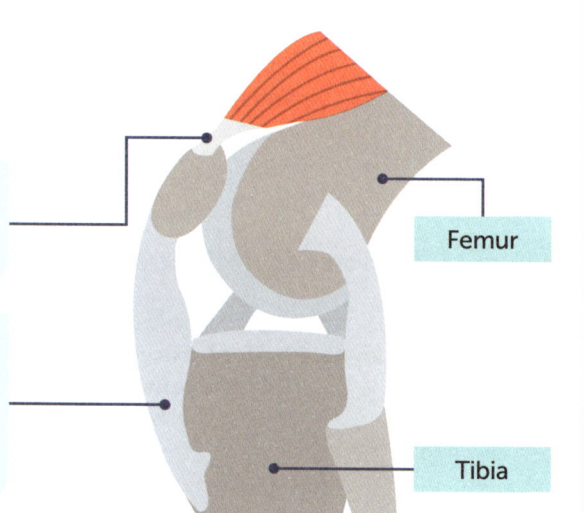

Femur

Tibia

The Achilles tendon is located at the back of the ankle. A tear of a tendon or ligament can take several weeks or months to heal.

David is a competitive rock climber. His shoulders, elbows and knees are in constant use. Describe the role of tendons and ligaments in the prevention of injury. [3]

Tendons connect muscles to bones[1] to absorb some impact as the muscles pull the bones when the muscle contracts.[1] Ligaments provide elasticity to absorb shock[1] / help keep the joint together by connecting bone to bone[1] / provide stability or restrict movement.[1]

CLASSIFICATION AND CHARACTERISTICS OF MUSCLE TYPES

The muscles of the body fall into three groups, each with a separate structure and function.

Voluntary muscles of the skeletal system

Skeletal muscles are under conscious control. We move them when we want to during sport and any other activity.

They are made of cylindrical fibres that attach to bones using tendons to create movement as they contract.

Involuntary muscles in blood vessels

Involuntary muscles do not require conscious control. They work automatically without any thought.

The muscles of the respiratory system constantly contract and relax to create a flow of air and oxygen into the lungs. **Smooth muscle** fibres in blood vessels contract and relax to narrow or widen the lumen (see **page 16**) in order control and distribute the flow of blood around the body during periods of rest and exercise.

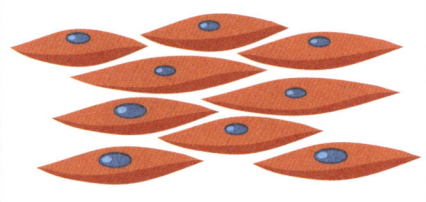

Cardiac muscle forming the heart

Cardiac muscle, found in the heart, is made of interconnected chains of fibres that can contract together to 'pump' the heart.

The heart rate is controlled through the regularity of contractions to increase or decrease the cardiac output (see **page 26**) to suit the intensity of exercise being undertaken.

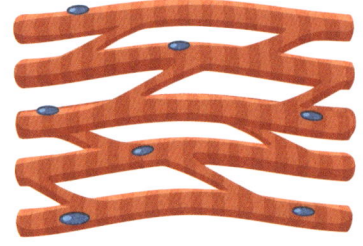

Explain, with the use of an example, why involuntary muscles in the blood vessels are important in the performance of sporting activity. [3]

> Muscles respond without any conscious effort[1] so that a performer can concentrate on their sport.[1] Blood vessels need to contract and relax for vascular shunting (see **page 17**) / to distribute more blood flow from the major organs to the muscles during exercise.[1]

1.1.8

LOCATION AND ROLE OF THE VOLUNTARY MUSCULAR SYSTEM

There are about 600 **muscles** in the human body.

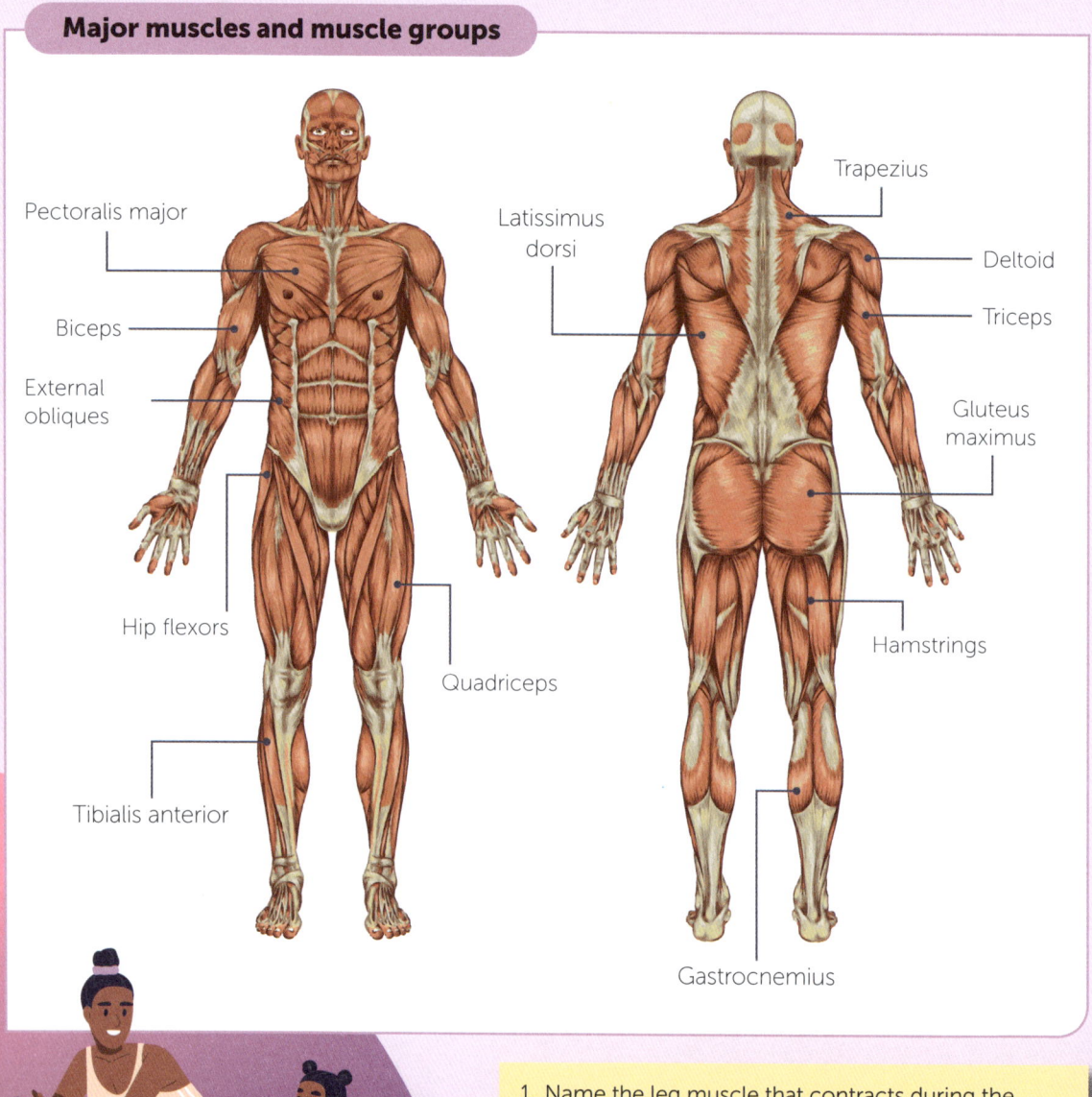

Major muscles and muscle groups

- Pectoralis major
- Biceps
- External obliques
- Hip flexors
- Quadriceps
- Tibialis anterior
- Latissimus dorsi
- Trapezius
- Deltoid
- Triceps
- Gluteus maximus
- Hamstrings
- Gastrocnemius

1. Name the leg muscle that contracts during the upward phase of a squat. [1]
2. Identify **one** muscle in the upper body that contracts to allow a performer to throw a ball. [1]

   1. Quadriceps.[1] (Or one of rectus femoris, vastus medialis, vastus lateralis, vastus intermedius.)
   2. Tricep,[1] pectoral,[1] deltoid.[1]

1.1.9

ANTAGONISTIC PAIRS OF MUSCLES

The major muscles of the body work in **antagonistic** pairs. As one muscle (the **agonist**) contracts to pull a bone, the opposite muscle (the **antagonist**) relaxes, to allow the bone to be pulled. This allows movements to take place and sporting actions to be executed.

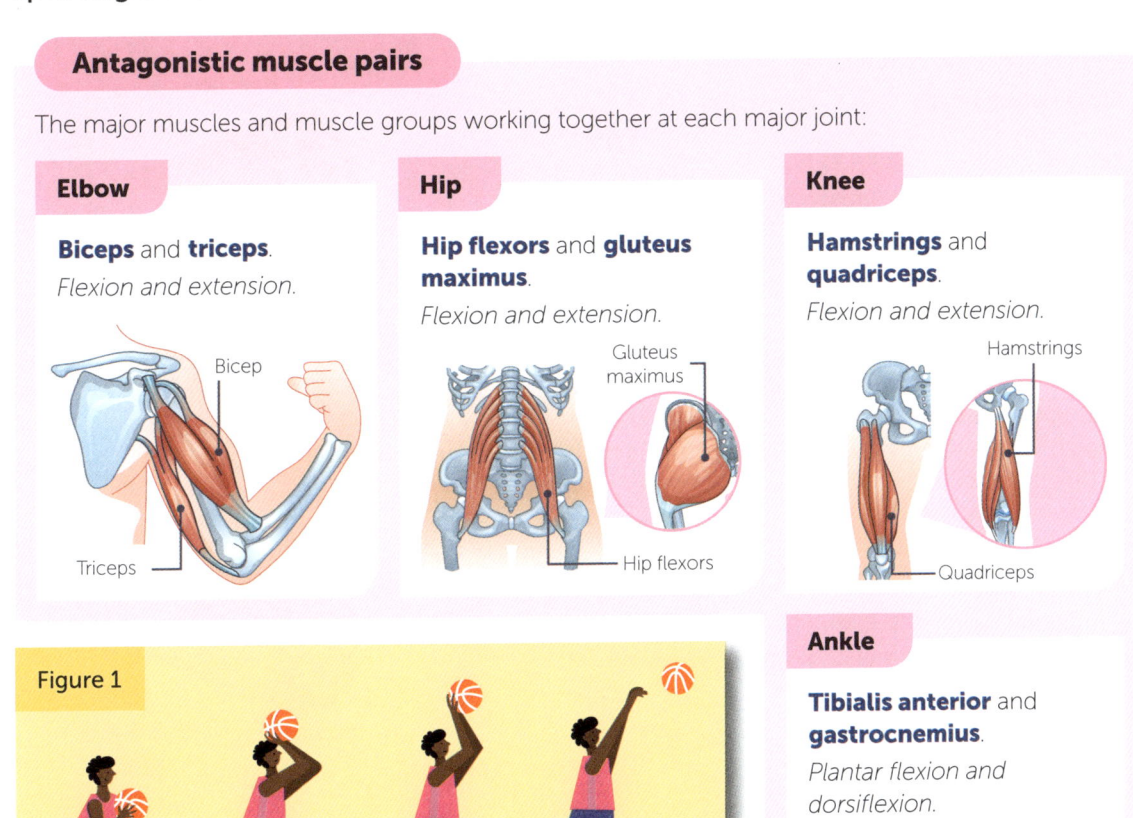

Antagonistic muscle pairs

The major muscles and muscle groups working together at each major joint:

Elbow

Biceps and **triceps**.
Flexion and extension.

Hip

Hip flexors and **gluteus maximus**.
Flexion and extension.

Knee

Hamstrings and **quadriceps**.
Flexion and extension.

Ankle

Tibialis anterior and **gastrocnemius**.
Plantar flexion and dorsiflexion.

Figure 1

Figure 1 shows a basketball player taking a free throw.
  (a) Name the agonist muscle and the antagonist muscle acting at the elbow when performing the throw. [2]
  (b) Name the agonist muscle and the antagonist muscle acting at the knee when performing the jump. [2]

(a) Agonist: triceps.[1] Antagonist: biceps.[1]
(b) Agonist: Quadriceps.[1] Antagonist: hamstrings.[1]

Agonists are the first muscle to start a movement (the **prime movers**). While the agonist (think pain and agony) contracts, the antagonist relaxes. The bicep may be the agonist in a pull-up, but the antagonist in a press-up.

Edexcel GCSE **Physical Education – Paper 1, Topic 1**

CHARACTERISTICS OF FAST AND SLOW TWITCH MUSCLE FIBRE TYPES

Voluntary muscles are made of elastic fibres which behave in different ways according to their make up and oxygen supply.

Slow twitch fibres (Type I)

Slow twitch fibres have a strong oxygen-rich blood supply making them redder in colour. These **Type I** fibres support aerobic activities such as long-distance running and endurance sports. They provide slower, less powerful contractions but they are much more resistant to fatigue than fast twitch fibres.

Fast twitch fibres (Types IIa and IIx)

Fast twitch fibres work well anaerobically (without oxygen). **Type IIx** muscles have the most powerful contractions which provide the largest amount of force for short bursts before they tire.

Type IIa fibres are a hybrid of Type I and Type IIx with aerobic and anaerobic characteristics. They are useful for sustained high intensity activity. Performers with more fast twitch fibres than slow twitch fibres tend to be best suited to sprinting and high energy sports.

Type I fibres

Type IIa fibres

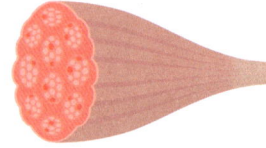
Type IIx fibres

People are born with a set percentage of slow and fast twitch fibres which make them naturally suited to some activities more than others.

The image below shows a long jumper in mid-flight. Explain which muscle fibre type is most likely to have been used in the legs when jumping from the take off board. [3]

Fast twitch type IIx[1] as this provides the greatest power for an explosive push off the board / supports a high intensity action.[1] The fibre contracts more quickly than other types of muscle fibre.[1]

HOW THE SKELETAL AND MUSCULAR SYSTEMS WORK TOGETHER

The skeleton and muscles form the **musculoskeletal system** which acts together to provide protection, posture, leverage and movement.

Protection

Bones are different shapes to provide protection for vital organs. They also bear the weight of the body and absorb impact. Bones are specific types of shape in order to fulfil their specialised roles. **See page 3**.

Posture

Muscles connect to bones in order to provide movement and to prevent the skeleton from collapsing. Muscles provide stability as well as movement. They also control our posture. **See page 10**.

Leverage

Bones provide a lever which can be pulled by muscles in order to create movement. **See page 30**.

Movement

Movement is controlled by muscles pulling on our bones. The connection of muscles and bones forms a joint. The type and power of movement at a joint is determined by the type of joint, the strength and type of muscle fibre contracting, the distance of the muscle from the pivot point (joint) and the force being exerted. **See pages 6, 11, 12 and 30**.

1.2.1

FUNCTIONS OF THE CARDIOVASCULAR SYSTEM

The cardiovascular system is responsible for the transport of oxygen, carbon dioxide and nutrients around the body, the clotting of open wounds, and the regulation of body temperature.

Transport of oxygen, carbon dioxide and nutrients

Oxygen, carbon dioxide and nutrients are transported through the bloodstream, suspended in plasma. A performer's working muscles require oxygen and the removal of waste carbon dioxide. Oxygen is required for muscles to work aerobically. **Lactic acid** can build up in muscles which also needs to be removed to the liver. Nutrients are carried to the working muscles to provide sufficient energy for them to continue the activity.

Blood clotting

Platelets control bleeding. They are carried in the bloodstream and rushed to any damaged areas of tissue in the body to plug the hole, forming a clot which can dry to form a scab. This helps to maintain blood pressure and the volume of blood within the body.

Regulation of body temperature

Blood flow is redistributed around the body in order to remove excess heat from the working muscles to other areas of the body. This prevents overheating which helps to maintain a peak level of performance and function.

Explain how the cardiovascular system helps to regulate an athlete's body temperature during their performance. [4]

During activity, work rate increases[1] which increases the temperature of the performer and their working muscles.[1] The body's CV system redistributes blood to increase flow to the working muscles to remove excess heat[1] by increasing the width of the arteries. Skin becomes red as a result of the dilation of blood vessels directly beneath it to reduce body temperature.[1]

1.2.2

STRUCTURE OF THE CARDIOVASCULAR SYSTEM

The **heart** is an organ that pumps blood around the body using a **double circulatory** system.

The heart

The heart has walls made of cardiac muscle with **four chambers** and four valves inside. The left and right sections are separated by the **septum** to ensure that oxygenated and deoxygenated blood do not mix.

The **right ventricle** pumps deoxygenated blood around the pulmonary loop to the lungs, where gas exchange takes place. (See **page 20**.) The **left ventricle** pumps blood around the rest of the body in the systemic loop. The **atria** collect blood as it returns to the heart and pump it into the ventricles. The atria contract just before the ventricles contract.

Oxygen-rich blood is carried away from the heart through **arteries**. Blood that has given up its oxygen to body cells is carried back to the heart through **veins** – it is deoxygenated. The blood shown as red has been oxygenated in the lungs. **Valves** between the atria and ventricles, and as the blood exits the heart, open and close with pressure, to prevent blood flowing backwards.

Complete the figure to show the pathway of the blood around the heart. [5]

Starting at the right ventricle, reorder statements 2–6 to show the pathway of the blood:

1. Deoxygenated blood fills the right atrium [1]
2. Then into the left ventricle through the bicuspid valve [ ]
3. Gas exchange occurs (blood is oxygenated) [ ]
4. It then flows into the right ventricle [ ]
5. Pulmonary vein transports oxygenated blood into the left atrium [ ]
6. The pulmonary artery then transports deoxygenated blood to the lungs [ ]
7. Oxygenated blood is ejected and transported to the body via the aorta. [7]

One mark for each statement in the correct order: 1, 4,[1] 6,[1] 3,[1] 5,[1] 2,[1] 7.

Double circulatory system of the heart

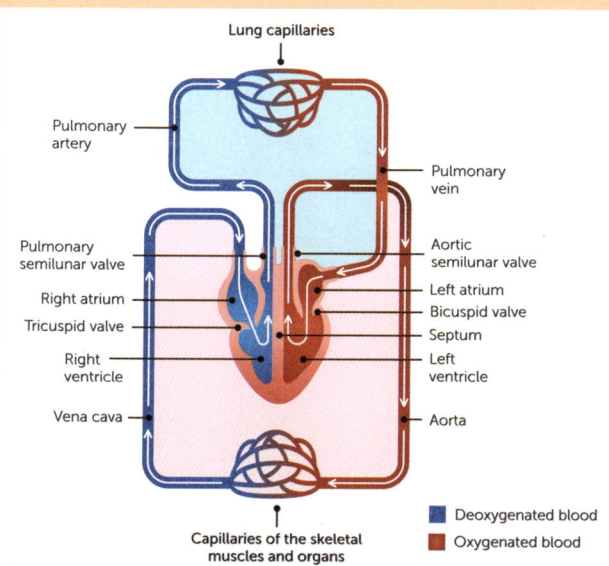

Edexcel GCSE **Physical Education – Paper 1, Topic 1**

BLOOD VESSELS, BLOOD FLOW AND BLOOD CELLS

The body contains three different types of blood vessel: **arteries**, **veins** and **capillaries**.

The aorta branches into different arteries that carry blood to the major organs. These branch more and more until they form tiny vessels within tissues called capillaries which wrap around muscles and organs. Capillaries then join up to form veins.

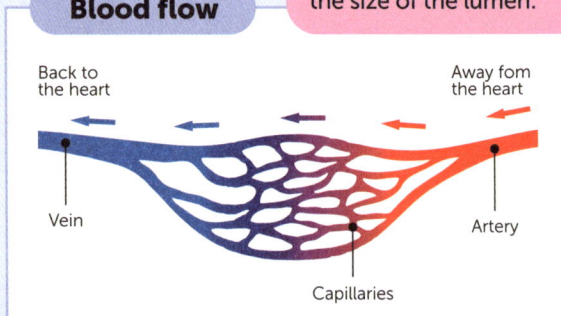

Note that the muscle in arteries does **NOT** pump blood, it simply adjusts the size of the lumen.

Blood vessel structure and function

	Arteries	Capillaries	Veins
Function	Carry oxygenated blood at high pressure away from the heart	Exchange of substances with cells	Return **deoxygenated** blood at low pressure to the heart
Lumen	Narrow to maintain pressure	Very narrow. Keeps red blood cells close to tissue cells	Large, so there is less resistance to blood flow
Wall	Elastic fibres stretch and recoil to maintain pressure. Thick wall resists bursting	Very thin – Short distance to maximise **gas exchange** by diffusion	Low pressure so no need for a thick elastic wall
Valve	No – High pressure blood keeps moving	No	Yes – Prevents backflow of low pressure blood

1. Define what is meant by a blood vessel. [1]
2. "All arteries carry oxygenated blood. All veins carry deoxygenated blood."
   Explain why this statement is not correct. [2]

   1. A tubular structure that carries blood around the body.[1]
   2. All arteries carry blood from the heart and veins carry it toward the heart[1] but the pulmonary vein carries oxygenated blood from the lungs to the heart / the pulmonary artery carries deoxygenated blood from the heart to the lungs.[1]

Redistribution of blood flow during exercise (Vascular shunting)

When exercising, the body redistributes blood to increase flow to the muscles that most need the oxygen it carries. This is known as the **vascular shunt** mechanism. The body increases the width of the lumen in the arteries, known as **vasodilation**, to increase flow to skeletal muscles.

Vasoconstriction is the term given to the narrowing of blood vessels to restrict blood flow to tissues and organs (such as the liver, gut and kidneys) that are not vital during maximal exercise. Shunting also transports more nutrients to the working muscles, removes more CO_2 and helps to reduce their temperature. Blood is shunted back to the organs when exercise pauses or stops.

When your blood pressure is monitored, a reading of 120/80 is considered healthy.

120 means the **systolic pressure** when the chambers of the heart eject blood to empty them. 80 is the **diastolic pressure** when the chambers relax to refill.

Red and white blood cells, platelets and plasma

Red blood cells
(Or erythrocytes) contain haemoglobin which enables them to carry oxygen. They also carry nutrients around the body. A large surface area increases the speed of diffusion (gas exchange) as they pass through the lungs.

White blood cells
Help us to fight infection and disease by killing viruses and bacteria, often using antibodies.

Plasma
Plasma comprises mostly water with additional salts and minerals. It suspends the blood cells and platelets within it to transport them around the body. Waste products such as urea and CO_2 (dissolved in its contents) are transported out of the body. Plasma also helps to regulate body temperature and blood pressure.

Platelets
Used to form blood clots in the event of an injury, cut or tear to the skin or internal organs. Platelets rush to the site of the wound and form a plug or clot. This can then form a scab.

During physical activity, blood pressure and volume is maintained through clotting if the wound is small enough to close naturally and a performer may play on, for example a rugby player injured in a tackle.

3. Give **one** role of red blood cells during exercise. [1]
4. The table, right, shows the redistribution of blood during exercise. Using the data in the table, analyse the redistribution of blood to the skeletal muscles during exercise. [1]

Destination	Rest	Maximal exercise
Skeletal muscles	19%	86%
Major organs	71%	8%
Skin	10%	6%

3. During exercise, the cells transport oxygen from the lungs to the working muscles of the body.[1] They also transport waste carbon dioxide (CO_2) from the muscles back to the lungs where it can be exhaled.[1]
4. It increases[1] (by 67%).

Edexcel GCSE **Physical Education** – Paper 1, Topic 1

COMPOSITION OF INHALED AND EXHALED AIR

The air we breathe

The composition of the air breathed in and out changes only in the oxygen and carbon dioxide content. The lungs absorb roughly 4% of the air as oxygen and exchange it for 4% carbon dioxide.

Inhaled air

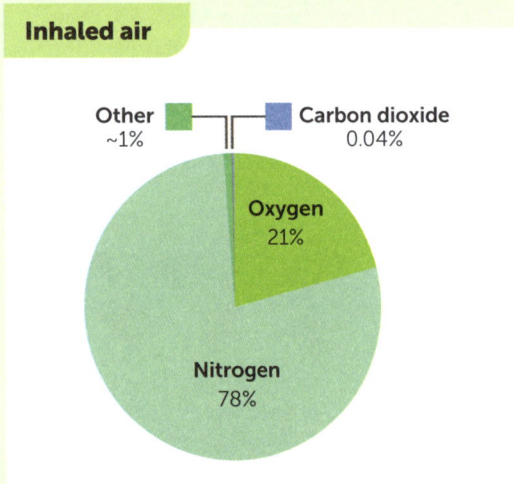

Exhaled air

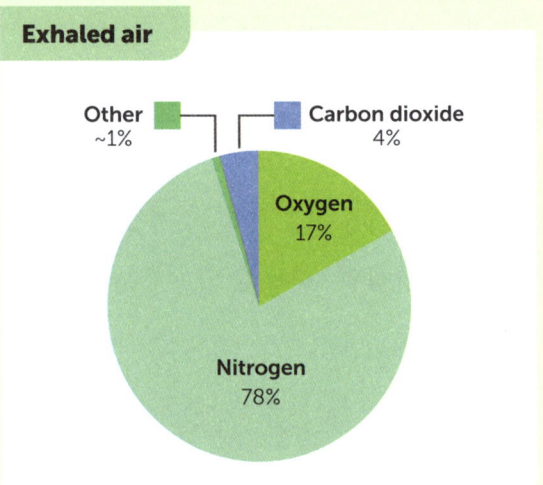

A distance swimmer has measured the percentages of air in their breath as shown in the diagrams above.

Explain **one** reason for the difference in the composition of air inhaled and exhaled in the diagrams. [2]

Oxygen is required[1] during aerobic exercise to provide the working muscles with their energy.[1] CO_2 is a waste product[1] formed through aerobic respiration of the working muscles during exercise.[1]

VITAL CAPACITY AND TIDAL VOLUME

A **spirometer** is a device used to measure different lung volumes, such as the amount of air inhaled or exhaled in a breath. A device reading is called a trace.

Lung volume measurements at rest and during exercise

Vital capacity

Vital capacity is the maximum volume of air that can forcefully be breathed in or out in one deep breath. This is usually about four litres.

Tidal volume

Tidal volume is the volume of air inhaled or exhaled per breath. At rest, tidal volume is approximately 500 ml.

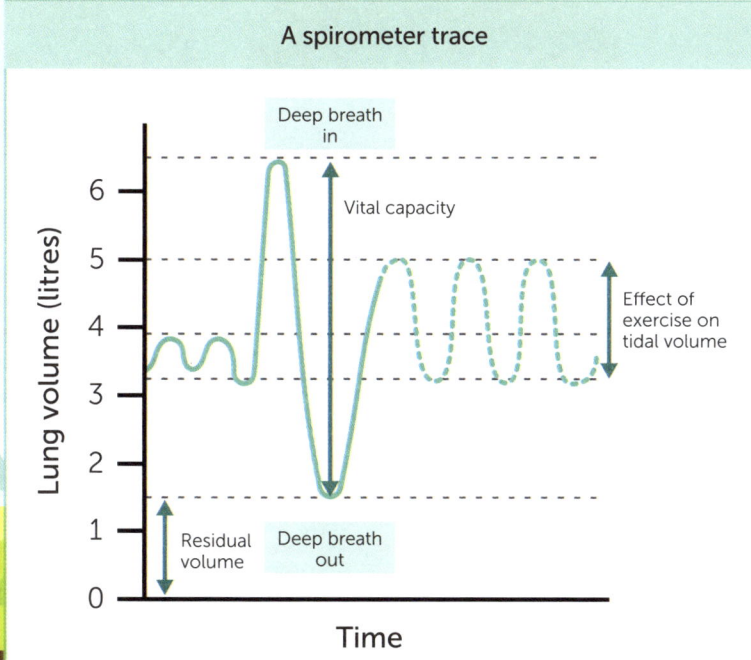

A spirometer trace

Tidal volume will increase during exercise in order to allow the body to consume more oxygen from the air to meet the energy demand.

Edexcel GCSE **Physical Education** – Paper 1, Topic 1

STRUCTURE AND FUNCTION OF THE RESPIRATORY SYSTEM

The pathway of air

1. As you breathe, air is drawn in through the **nose or mouth** into the **trachea**.
2. It passes into the **bronchi**,
3. And branches into the smaller **bronchioles**,
4. Which fills the **lungs**,
5. Where oxygen is diffused into the blood via smaller air sacs called **alveoli**.

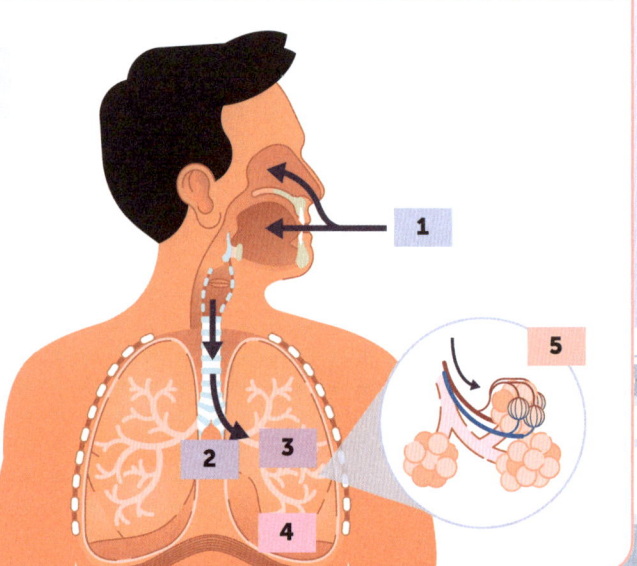

Gaseous exchange

The **alveoli** provide a very large surface area with **moist**, **thin** walls only **one cell thick**. This makes **diffusion** easier as the distance across one cell is so short. Lots of blood **capillaries** create a **strong blood supply** for the oxygen to diffuse into.

Two gases diffusing in opposite directions at the same time is called **gaseous exchange**. **Oxygen concentration** is lower in the capillaries than it is in the alveoli, so it passes through the capillary membrane into the blood as a result of diffusion. **Carbon dioxide** in the capillaries is in greater concentration than in the alveoli so it passes back through the other way into the lungs to be exhaled.

Oxygen combines with **haemoglobin** in the red blood cells to form **oxyhaemoglobin**. Haemoglobin can also carry carbon dioxide.

Gaseous exchange also takes place in the muscles where oxygen passes from the bloodstream to the muscles.

1. Explain how oxygen and carbon dioxide swap between the lungs and the bloodstream. [2]

1. The concentration of each gas will try equalise on both sides of the alveolo–capillary membrane[1] so where there is greater concentration of one gas on one side, some will pass through to provide more oxygen in the blood or to remove excess carbon dioxide.[1]

The role of respiratory muscles in breathing

Changes in air pressure cause inhalation and exhalation. The rate of inhalation and exhalation can be controlled through the use of chest and abdominal muscles such as the **rib cage**, **intercostal muscles** (those between the ribs) and the **diaphragm**.

When inhaling, negative air pressure is created within the lungs to draw in a breath of air. Air always moves from areas of high pressure to areas of low pressure to create an equilibrium of pressure.

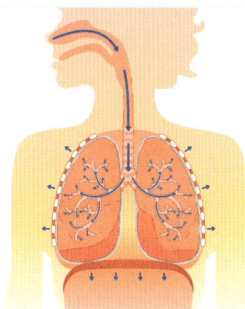

Inhalation

1. The diaphragm contracts, moving downwards from a dome shape to a flatter shape.
2. The intercostal muscles contract moving the rib cage up and out.
3. This increases the volume inside the chest cavity;
4. Which decreases the pressure inside the chest cavity.
5. A pressure gradient is created, pulling air into the lungs through the nose or mouth.

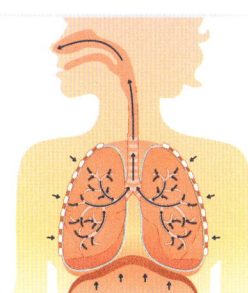

Exhalation

1. The diaphragm relaxes and returns to a dome shape.
2. The intercostal muscles relax moving the rib cage down and in.
3. This decreases the volume inside the chest cavity;
4. Which increases the pressure inside the chest cavity.
5. A pressure gradient is created and air is pushed out.

The effect of exercise on breathing

During exercise, inhalation and exhalation need to happen more quickly to allow the lungs to diffuse more oxygen into the bloodstream. The lungs can also expand more during **inspiration** (breathing in) with the use of the **sternocleidomastoid** and **pectoral muscles**. During **expiration** (breathing out), the rib cage is pulled down to force air out more quickly with use of the **abdominal muscles**.

2. Complete the table by adding **one** tick to each row to show how each of the following skeletal muscles help in the breathing process during exercise. [3]

Muscle	Helps with inhalation?	Helps with exhalation?
Abdominals		
Pectoral muscles		

2. Inhalation: pectoral muscles.[1] Exhalation: abdominals.[1]

HOW THE CARDIOVASCULAR AND RESPIRATORY SYSTEMS WORK TOGETHER

The cardiovascular system refers to the heart and the circulation of blood through the blood vessels. The respiratory system refers to the lungs and oxygen exchange processes. Together they form the cardio-respiratory system.

Cardio-respiratory system

The **respiratory system** draws in and absorbs oxygen into the blood stream for the **cardiovascular system** to pass around the body to the muscles and organs.

During aerobic exercise, the **cardio-respiratory system** works harder to provide sufficient oxygen to the working muscles and to remove the additional carbon dioxide produced by them to avoid fatigue.

Oxygen deficit

Excess post-exercise oxygen consumption or **EPOC** refers to continued heavy breathing or increased tidal volume once exercise has finished. This is also known as **repaying the oxygen debt**.

During vigorous exercise, the muscles respire anaerobically, producing lactic acid and creating an oxygen deficit. This is as a result of having insufficient oxygen. After exercise, the debt of oxygen that has built up is repaid by maintaining a high breathing rate. The elevated level of oxygen helps to remove lactic acid by converting it back into glucose, and subsequently into CO_2 and water.

The recovery process from vigorous exercise

Cooling down after exercise with a few minutes of light physical activity helps to maintain an elevated breathing rate and heart rate (blood flow). This eases the body out of exercise and provides continued blood flow and increased oxygen to the active muscles, which helps with the removal of **lactic acid**.

As a result of dynamic work, muscles will have contracted and increased in tension. Stretching encourages them to return to their resting length and reduces stiffness and soreness.

Describe how a footballer could aide their recovery after an intense match. [4]

Answer may include: Cool down with light exercise[1] to slowly lower the heart rate to normal.[1] Drink plenty of water to rehydrate,[1] replacing water[1] and minerals lost through sweat. Take an ice bath[1] to reduce muscle soreness.[1] Gently stretch[1] while the muscles are still warm.[1] Eat simple carbohydrates[1] to replenish glycogen stores.[1]

1.3.1 | 1.3.2

AEROBIC AND ANAEROBIC EXERCISE

Aerobic exercise means being in the presence of, or using oxygen. **Anaerobic exercise** means it is done in the absence of (enough) oxygen.

Aerobic exercise

Aerobic capacity is the ability to take in and transfer oxygen to the working muscles in order to exercise continuously without tiring. During **aerobic exercise**, like marathon running, the relatively **low intensity** of the activity should allow for the heart and lungs to provide enough oxygen for the muscles to use as they work. As a result, the activity can be sustained for a **long period** of time. Examples include:

- Marathon running
- 2000m rowing
- Distance cycling
- Gentle skipping

Oxygen mixes with the **glucose** in the body to release energy to fuel muscle movement. Waste products are **water** (sweat) and **carbon dioxide** (through increased exhalation).

Summary of aerobic exercise:

(glucose + oxygen →
energy + carbon dioxide + water)

The **duration** and/or **intensity** of a physical activity generally determine if it is aerobic or anaerobic.

Anaerobic exercise

During **anaerobic** exercise, like sprinting, the **high intensity** of the activity doesn't allow the heart and lungs to provide enough oxygen for the muscles to use as they work. The activity is too intense for delivery to keep up with demand. As a result, muscles are forced to work without enough oxygen and **lactic acid** is produced as a waste product. The lactic acid causes pain and fatigue so these activities can only be sustained for a **short period** of time. Examples include:

- Sprinting
- Heavy weightlifting
- Cycling sprints
- Long jump

Summary of anaerobic exercise:

(glucose → energy + lactic acid)

Energy sources

Fats act as a fuel source for aerobic activity.

Carbohydrates act as a fuel source for both aerobic and anaerobic activity.

Discuss whether swimming should be considered aerobic or anaerobic. [6]

A 10k swim would be performed over a long period of time[✓] with moderate exertion throughout and little or no opportunity to rest[✓] which is aerobic.[✓] Sufficient oxygen would be available for energy to be produced to maintain muscle contractions.[✓]

A competitive 50m race would be of high intensity and could not be sustained for long.[✓] Lactic acid would be produced by the muscles owing to a lack of oxygen[✓] which is anaerobic[✓] as the blood uses its own blood sugar and/or glycogen stores as an alternative energy source.[✓]

Depending on the intensity of the swimming, and the duration it is done for, it could be either.[✓]

This question should be marked in accordance with the levels of response guidance on page 123.

1.4.1 1.4.2 1.4.3

THE SHORT-TERM EFFECTS OF EXERCISE

The effects of exercise on muscles and bones, the heart and the respiratory system depend on the period over which activity is undertaken.

Short-term effects of exercise on the body

Lactate accumulation

Working muscles produce **blood lactate** (**lactic acid**) and carbon dioxide as waste products during vigorous (anaerobic) exercise as a result of insufficient oxygen. Increased blood flow improves the supply of oxygen to the muscles to reduce the build up of lactic acid and also helps to carry away lactic acid and CO_2 that has already accumulated. Lactic acid causes fatigue in the muscles which is experienced as pain and discomfort, reducing performance and causing the heart rate to stay higher than normal.

Muscle fatigue

The working muscles demand more oxygen-rich blood during exercise. In response to this demand, the heart works harder to pump blood to the working muscles more quickly, and blood pressure increases. **Vascular shunting** (see **page 17**) also redirects blood to the muscles during exercise and reduces the flow to the major organs to a minimal level.

If the muscles do not receive sufficient blood oxygen, they begin to work anaerobically and **fatigue** quickly sets in. The muscles also require the waste carbon dioxide to be removed as quickly as it is produced to avoid fatigue.

Muscle temperature

Muscles generate heat as they create energy. Exercise also increases blood flow to the working muscles, increasing their temperature. Warming muscles makes them more **elastic** so that they are more likely to stretch rather than **tear**.

Increased depth of breathing

Exercise causes the **respiratory rate**, **tidal volume** and **minute ventilation** to increase. The increase in the depth and frequency of breathing happens to bring more air (and therefore oxygen) into the lungs to oxygenate the blood more quickly. Increased exhalation also removes waste carbon dioxide more quickly.

> Heart rate, stroke volume and cardiac output will increase during exercise. See page 26.

Figure 1 below shows the respiratory rate of a rugby player before, during and after a match.

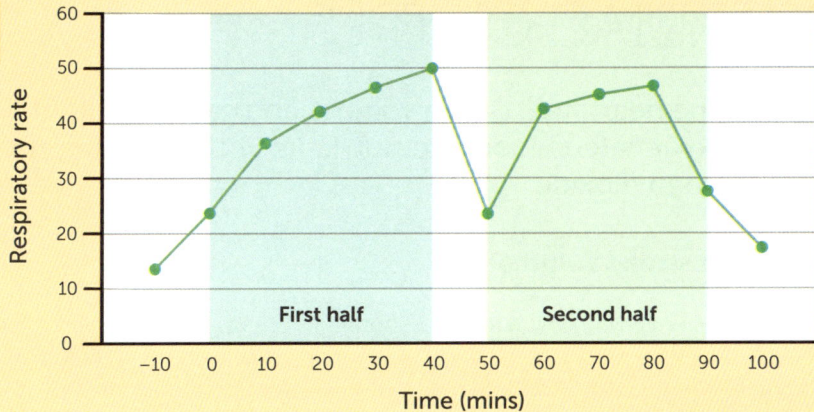

Figure 1

(a) Using the information in the graph, analyse how the respiratory rates compare in the first half and second half of the game and give reasons for their difference. [3]
(b) Explain why the respiratory rate dropped significantly between 40 and 50 minutes. [1]

(a) First half became more intense than the second half.[1] First half got gradually more intense as the match progressed but the second half was consistently intense until the last 10 minutes.[1] Performance in the first half was intense until the whistle but the second half tailed off 10 minutes before the end.[1] This may be caused by a change in team possession of the ball / change of strategy / decline in motivation / tiredness / injury / time in the sin bin.[1]

(b) Half time break so the player had a lower demand for oxygen.[1]

! Note

Specification point 1.4.4 is covered on **page 22**.
Point 1.4.5 is covered on **pages 51–53**.

1.4.6

HEART RATE, STROKE VOLUME AND CARDIAC OUTPUT

During exercise, the heart rate, stroke volume and cardiac output will increase to pump newly oxygenated blood and nutrients to the working muscles and remove waste carbon dioxide.

Heart rate and stroke volume

Heart rate is the frequency with which the heart contracts (beats). It is measured in **beats per minute**. The natural resting heart rate is controlled by a group of cells found in the right atrium. They act as a pacemaker, producing regular impulses that travel through the heart causing it to contract.

Heart rate naturally increases during exercise to supply the muscles with the additional oxygen they need. Before exercise, adrenaline will cause the heart rate to rise in anticipation.

Stroke volume is the volume of blood pumped out of the heart by the left ventricle with one contraction.

Cardiac output

The volume of blood pumped by each ventricle of the heart in one minute is called the **cardiac output**. It is calculated as the product of **stroke volume** and the **heart rate**.

Cardiac output (Q) = stroke volume (mL) × heart rate (beats per minute)

1. A person has a resting stroke volume of 60 ml/beat and a heart rate of 65 beats per minute (bpm). Calculate the cardiac output. [2]
2. The following heart rate graph shows the data from a cyclist's training session.
   (a) Explain why the heart rate increased before exercise began at 8 mins. [2]
   (b) Suggest what might have caused a changed in heart rate at 13 mins and 17 mins. [1]

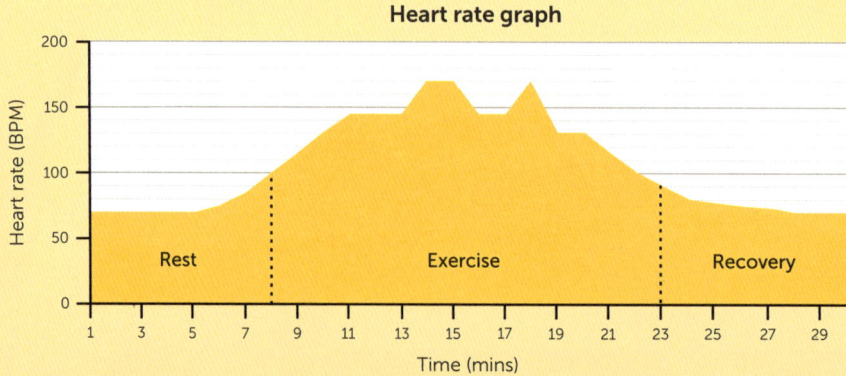

1. 60 × 65 = 3900[1] mL per minute / 3.9 litres per minute.[1]
2. (a) Before exercise, adrenaline[1] will cause an anticipatory[1] rise in heart rate.
   (b) A hill / change in resistance[1] could create an increase in exertion.

Paper 1, Topic 1

EXAMINATION PRACTICE

1. Which **one** of the following bones is located at the hip? [1]
   - ☐ A – Femur
   - ☐ B – Scapula
   - ☐ C – Talus
   - ☐ D – Tibia

2. Which **one** of these statements defines abduction at the shoulder? [1]
   - ☐ A – A rotational movement of the humerus
   - ☐ B – A contraction of the deltoid
   - ☐ C – Raising the arms above the head
   - ☐ D – The movement of an arm away from the midline of the body

3. Which **one** of the following is a region of the spinal column? [1]
   - ☐ A – Carpal
   - ☐ B – Cervical
   - ☐ C – Clavicle
   - ☐ D – Cranium

4. Which **one** of the following is a short term effect of exercise? [1]
   - ☐ A – Improved muscular endurance
   - ☐ B – Improved speed
   - ☐ C – Increased heart rate
   - ☐ D – Increased size of the heart

5. Blood flows around the body in a double circulatory system.
   Which **one** of the following describes the correct pathway of the blood as it enters the heart via the pulmonary vein? [1]
   - ☐ A – Left atrium → left ventricle → right atrium → right ventricle
   - ☐ B – Left atrium → right atrium → left ventricle → right atrium
   - ☐ C – Right atrium → right ventricle → left atrium → left ventricle
   - ☐ D – Right ventricle → left ventricle → right atrium → left atrium

6. Bones produce blood cells and platelets. White blood cells fight infection.
   Complete the following statements:
   (a) Blood platelets are responsible for _____ in the event of injury. [1]
   (b) Red blood cells carry _____ around the body. [1]

7. Give **three** functions of the skeleton. [3]

8. Tendons and ligaments are found at major synovial joints.
   Explain **two** differences between tendons and ligaments. [2]

9. Lee conducts a press up into a high plank position.

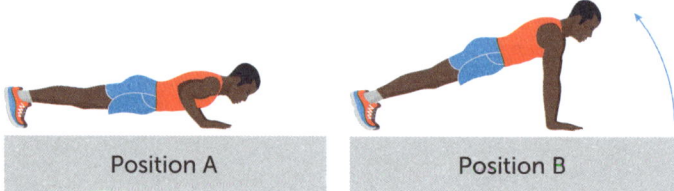

Identify the working muscle in the arm above the elbow responsible for the movement from position A to position B. [1]

10. The ankle is made up of short bones.

Figure 1

Explain the importance of having short bones in the ankle for a basketball player in **Figure 1**. [2]

11. **Figure 2** shows a footballer performing a throw in.

Figure 2

(a) Complete the table below to:
  (i) State the type of joints labelled A and B at the neck and wrist. [2]
  (ii) Give **one** example of the range of movement at each joint. [2]

Joint	Classification of joint	Range of movement possible
Neck (A)		
Wrist (B)		

(b) Explain how the function of the cranium assists the performance of the football player. [2]
(c) The player is using voluntary skeletal muscles to perform the throw in.
Explain why voluntary muscles are important to the player in their performance. [2]
(d) Analyse the use of type IIx muscle fibres used in performing the throw in. [3]

12 Petra takes a free throw shot in basketball.
  (a) Describe how muscles and bones work together to produce movement. [3]

Petra's tidal volume was monitored for one minute before and after the game starts.
A graph is shown below.

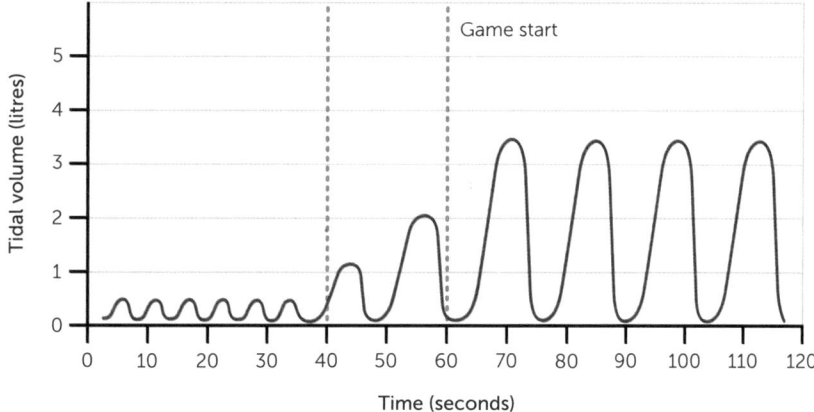

(b) Define what is meant by tidal volume. [1]
(c) At 60 seconds, Petra walks onto the court to play. Explain the effect of exercise on her tidal volume. [1]
(d) Explain why Petra's tidal volume may have started to change after 40 seconds. [1]
(e) Name **one** muscle that helps Petra's diaphragm to take a deeper breath when she needs it during intense exercise. [1]

When Petra takes a breath, air is drawn into her lungs to the alveoli.
(f) Describe the function of the alveoli. [3]
(g) Give **one** advantage to Petra of increasing her aerobic capacity. [1]
(h) State the main fuel source for anaerobic activity. [1]

LEVER SYSTEMS

There are three classes of lever system in the body. Each lever system has a fulcrum, load and effort.

Fulcrums, load and effort

Levers involve a rigid bar (bone) that pivots or rotates about a fulcrum (joint) with a load applied. A lever system comprises:

- A **fulcrum** or pivot around which a force is exerted. (In the body, this is a joint.)
- A **load** (or **resistance**) being moved. (In the body this relates to bodyweight and any additional load being carried.)
- The **effort** or force required to move the load. (Muscular effort.)

First, second and third class lever systems

First class lever

First class levers have the fulcrum between the effort and the load or resistance, like a see-saw.

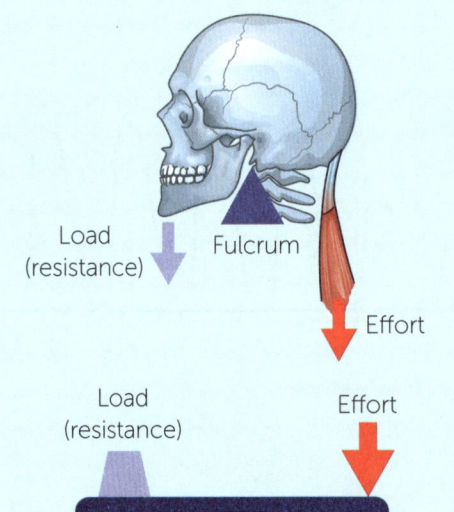

A football player heads a ball using a class 1 lever action in a Serie A Juventus game.

1. Complete the statement: The type of lever system working at the knee in the upward phase of a squat is an example of a _____. [1]

2. Identify the lever system that is used to go up onto the toes when pushing off the blocks in a sprint start. [1]

   1. Third class lever.[1]
   2. Second class lever.[1]

FLE 123 is a useful mnemonic to remember the lever classes.
A class 1 has the *Fulcrum* (*pivot*) in the middle.
A class 2 has the *Load* (*resistance*) in the middle
A class 3 has the *Effort* (*force*) in the middle.

First, second and third class lever systems continued

Second class lever

Second class levers are most easily remembered as having a wheelbarrow action. The fulcrum is at one end with the effort at the opposite end. The load or resistance is anywhere in the middle.

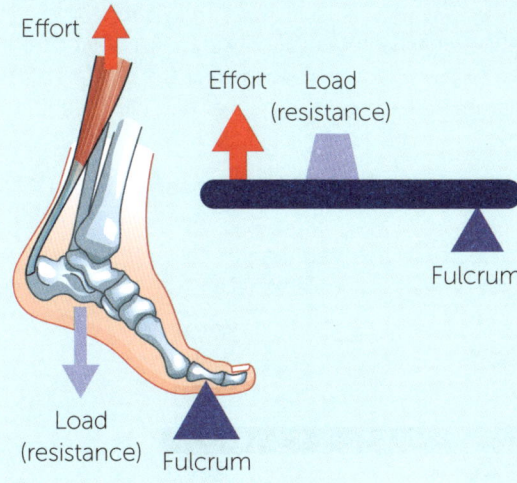

An athlete takes advantage of a class 2 lever action with plantar flexion at the ankle to leave the take off board with explosive power at a long jump event.

> Think about where the muscle attaches to the bone when considering what type of lever system applies to an action.

Third class lever

A class 3 lever has the fulcrum at one end, the load at the opposite end and the effort applied in the middle.

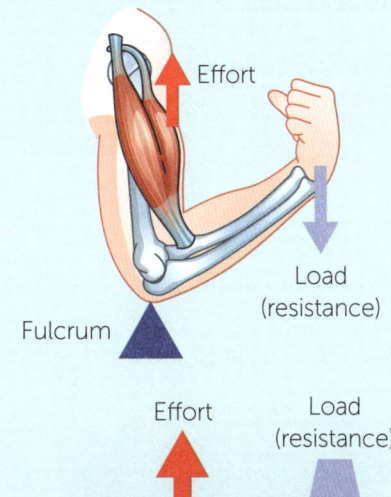

A GB rower uses his biceps to flex at the elbow in a class 3 lever action to draw the paddle through the water in the Men's Kayak Sprint 200m at the Olympic Games in Rio.

Edexcel GCSE **Physical Education** – Paper 1, Topic 2

2.1.2

MECHANICAL ADVANTAGE AND DISADVANTAGE

A lever is a very simple way to gain mechanical advantage (MA), creating the ability to lift a heavy load with relatively small muscular effort.

Calculating mechanical advantage

A lever has a mechanical advantage if its effort arm is longer than its load arm. By comparing the distance of the effort and the load from the fulcrum, you can determine the degree of mechanical advantage. A lever with mechanical advantage is a more efficient lever and will be able to move heavier loads with relatively little effort.

Mechanical advantage = effort arm ÷ weight (resistance/load) arm

A **first class lever** must have the fulcrum nearer to the load than the effort for it to have a mechanical advantage. The nearer it is, the greater the advantage.

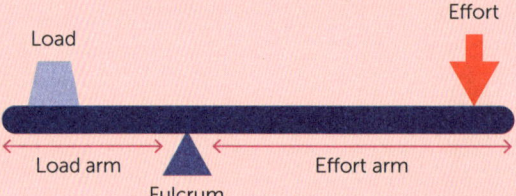

A **second class lever** always has a mechanical advantage of greater than 1 as the effort is always further from the fulcrum than the load. This means a heavy load can be lifted more efficiently.

A **third class lever** is said to have a **mechanical disadvantage** as the effort is always closer to the fulcrum than the load. Despite a mechanical disadvantage when it comes to load, class 3 levers increase distance, so a short muscle movement produces a greater output movement. The hip joint is an example of a class 3 lever, producing large movements of the femur with a relatively small movement near the fulcrum (ball joint).

A tennis player makes a backhand volley.
  (a) Identify the type of lever acting in the extension of the elbow during the stroke. [1]
  (b) Explain the mechanical advantage or disadvantage of this lever system. [3]

(a) First class lever.[1]
(b) A mechanical disadvantage occurs[1] as the effort (tricep muscle) is closer to the fulcrum[1] (elbow) than the load[1] (tennis racket in the hand at the end of the forearm). However, a short tricep movement creates a large forearm movement to hit the ball with force.[1]

MOVEMENT PATTERNS USING BODY PLANES AND AXES

There are three planes and three axes of movement used whilst performing sporting actions.

Planes and axes

A **plane** of movement is an imaginary flat surface across which the body moves in an action. An **axis** of movement is an imaginary line through the body, about which the body rotates.

> Movements occur *in* a plane and *around* an axis, so the plane and the axis for a movement should be revised together as pairs.

Sagittal & frontal

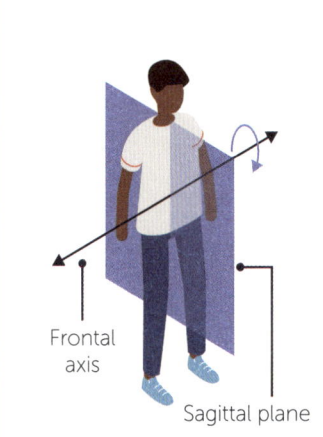

Frontal axis
Sagittal plane

Typical movements

Running, flexion and extension actions take place in the **sagittal plane**.

Bending and rolling actions take place around the **frontal axis**.

Frontal & sagittal

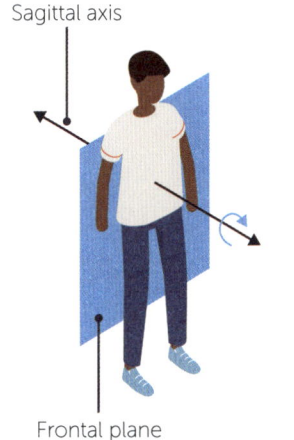

Sagittal axis
Frontal plane

Typical movements

Sidestepping and sideways adduction and abduction use the **frontal plane**.

Cartwheels take place around the **sagittal axis**.

Transverse & vertical

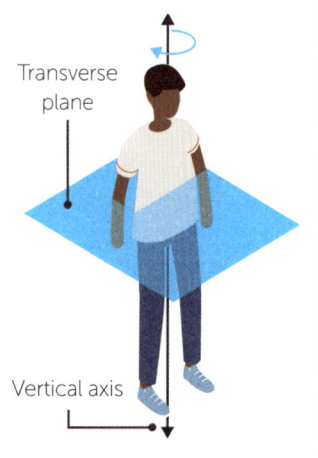

Transverse plane
Vertical axis

Typical movements

Twisting, rotating or spinning actions happen in the **transverse plane**.

Spinning and pivoting happen around the **vertical axis**.

A trampoline gymnast performs a full standing twist.
  (a) Identify the plane and axis of movement used in performing a full twist. [2]
  (b) Identify another sporting action that uses the same plane and axis of rotation. [1]

  (a) Transverse plane.[1] Vertical axis.[1]
  (b) Answer may include: 360 jump in skiing/snowboarding,[1] spin in ice skating,[1] pirouette in dance,[1] twist in trampolining,[1] spinning kick in martial arts.[1]

Paper 1, Topic 2

EXAMINATION PRACTICE

1. **Figure 1** shows a rugby player about to make a conversion.

Figure 1

   Which **one** of the following lever systems is acting at the knee to kick the ball? [1]
   - ☐ A – First class lever
   - ☐ B – Second class lever
   - ☐ C – Third class lever
   - ☐ D – Both A and B

2. Which **one** of the following lever systems would result in mechanical advantage? [1]
   - ☐ A – A longer load arm than effort arm
   - ☐ B – The effort closer to the fulcrum than the load
   - ☐ C – The fulcrum centred in between the load and the effort
   - ☐ D – The load in between the effort and the fulcrum

3. **Figure 2** shows a diagram of a diver performing a piked somersault.
   (a) State the plane and axis of movement used in the somersault. [2]

Figure 2

   (b) Identify the class of lever acting at the ankle on take-off. [1]
   (c) Draw a fully labelled diagram to show the class of lever identified in part (b). [2]
   (d) Explain why a class three lever has no mechanical advantage. [2]

34 ClearRevise

3.1 HEALTH AND FITNESS

Health and fitness are related but they are not the same thing. Exercise plays a role in both.

Health

Health is defined as **a person's complete state of emotional, social and physical well-being and not just the absence of disease.** All physiological systems need to be in positive, balanced harmony.

Decreased health may affect the intensity, regularity and desire to train or exercise, lowering fitness.

Fitness

Fitness describes **a person's ability to effectively meet or cope with the demands of their physical environment**. They should be able to physically perform an activity or task without increased risk of injury.

Fitness can still be increased despite poor health, for example if someone has an unhealthy diet, but is still able to train.

Exercise

Exercise can improve health, and appropriate levels can improve **performance**. Too much exercise can be negative.

- Exercise can cause a drop in resting blood pressure, improving physical health and reducing the risk of heart disease.
- Exercise can help people to temporarily forget about their worries, improving social health and reducing anxiety.
- Exercise can involve teamwork and companionship, improving social health.

See **page 69** for more details.

Mohammed said that "Abdi is healthy because he is not physically ill or frail".

(a) Explain what is incorrect about this statement. [2]

(b) Give **two** ways that health may be improved through greater fitness. [2]

(a) Abdi could have low self esteem / stress / depression / suffer from loneliness / poor posture / high blood pressure / alcohol or drug abuse / smoking habit / poor diet[1] which may not impact his physical condition / impacts his complete state of well-being.[1]

(b) Answers may include two from: Reduced chance of illness and disease / better sleep patterns / improved posture and personal image / stronger heart and reduced risk of heart disease / lower blood pressure / reduced risk of diabetes through reduced body fat / better social life if training together with others.

Edexcel GCSE Physical Education – Paper 1, Topic 3

THE COMPONENTS OF FITNESS

Each of the components of fitness can be linked to various sports. They can help to plan, carry out, monitor and evaluate exercise and training programmes to suit individual needs.

Agility – The ability to move and change direction quickly (at speed) whilst maintaining control.

Rugby players need agility to side step around opposing defence players to avoid a tackle and gain territory.

Cardiovascular fitness / aerobic endurance – The ability of the heart and lungs to supply oxygen to the working muscles.

Marathon and endurance runners need to be able to maintain a high volume of oxygenated blood to the working muscles for a long period.

Muscular endurance – The ability of a muscle or muscle group to undergo repeated contractions, without fatigue.

Triathletes require muscular endurance for running, swimming and cycling to reduce fatigue in muscles repeatedly contracting.

Balance – The maintenance of the centre of mass over the base of support. Balance may be static (still) or dynamic (whilst moving).

Windsurfers and **horse riders** need excellent balance to continually adjust their centre of mass to stay on top of their boards or horses as they move.

Coordination – The ability to use two or more body parts together smoothly and efficiently.

Ball and racket sports require excellent hand, eye and body coordination in order to strike the ball cleanly on a consistent basis.

Flexibility – The range of movements possible at a joint.

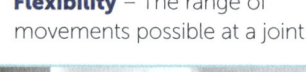

Gymnasts, **divers**, **martial artists** and **figure skaters** require excellent flexibility to increase their range of movement and to reduce injury.

Reaction time – The time taken to initiate a response to a stimulus.

Sprint racers need to react to a starting gun quickly. **Boxers** need to avoid punches.

Speed – The ability to move body parts to perform an action quickly.

Sprinters and **tennis players** require speed to move quickly across the track or court.

Strength – The ability to overcome a resistance (maximal, static, dynamic and explosive): **Maximal strength** is the absolute maximum force that can be generated in one muscle contraction. **Static strength** is the ability to hold a body part or limb in a still position. **Dynamic strength** is the ability to apply force when the muscles are continually contracting and extending. **Explosive strength** (**power**) is the product of strength and speed, i.e. strength × speed.

High maximal strength is required in **boxing** and **weightlifting**.

Static strength helps **rugby** players to hold the resistance in a scrum position.

Gymnasts have high dynamic strength.

Explosive strength (power), is crucial in **sprint sports**, **boxing**, **shot put** and **volleyball** to provide bursts of power when needed. For example, to get out of the blocks first, create a final burst to the finish line, put a shot or smash a ball with strength and speed.

Body composition – The percentages fat, muscle and bone in the human body.

Rock climbers will favour a leaner body composition with a low percentage of fat. **Shot putters** benefit from increased body mass.

The value of fitness testing

Fitness testing allows performers and coaches to:

- identify strengths and/or weaknesses in a performance or the success of a training programme
- monitor improvement
- show a starting level of fitness
- inform training requirements
- compare against norms of the group, previous results and national averages
- check for progress
- motivate and set goals
- provide variety in a training programme.

Explain how a rock climber would require high static and dynamic strength. [2]

Static strength is required in hand holds / grip strength when holding their weight / foot holds when standing on a ledge.[1] Dynamic strength is necessary to repeatedly lift their own weight when moving up the rock face / leaping and securing a hold.[1]

| 3.2.2 | 3.2.3 | 3.2.4 |

FITNESS TESTS

Each of the components of fitness can be linked to various sports and can help to plan, carry out, monitor and evaluate exercise and training programmes to suit individual needs.

Cardiovascular fitness (stamina)

Cardiovascular fitness or **stamina** is the ability of the heart and lungs to supply oxygen to the working muscles. It can be measured using the Cooper 12 minute run/swim test or the Harvard step test.

Marathon and **endurance runners** need stamina to be able to maintain a high volume of oxygenated blood to the working muscles for a long period.

Cooper 12 minute run/swim test

Participants of the Cooper test aim to cover as much distance as they can in 12 minutes using a **track** (or pool), some **distance markers**, **recording sheets** and a **stopwatch**. Distance is usually measured in kilometres or miles. The test can be carried out on multiple people at the same time.

Expected performance is based on gender and age, but range between a score of 'Excellent' over 2800 metres for a male in his twenties, and a score of 'Poor' with 1100 metres for a woman in her fifties.

Harvard step test

A **bench** and a **timer** is required for this test.

Participants of the Harvard step test should step on and off a standard gym bench once every two seconds for five minutes. Their pulse should be measured one minute after finishing, and again at two and three minutes after finishing. The score is calculated as:

$$30{,}000 \div (\text{Pulse 1} + \text{Pulse 2} + \text{Pulse 3}).$$

1. The normative data for the Harvard step test (age 16) is provided below.

Gender	Excellent	Above average	Average	Below average	Poor
Male	> 90.0	80.0–90.0	65.0–79.9	55.0–64.9	< 55
Female	> 86.0	76.0–86.0	61.0–75.9	50.0–60.9	< 50

Jim scored 79.4 in his most recent step test. Ellie scored 76.2.

(a) Evaluate the performance of Jim and Ellie. [3]

(b) Ellie tested again each month for three months. Her scores were 78.1, 80.3 and most recently 81.8. Predict her next score if she continued to test again next month. [1]

(a) Jim is average.[1] Ellie is above average.[1] Even though Jim's score was better, his comparative performance as a male was not as good as Ellie.[1] Ellie has better cardiovascular fitness than Jim.[1]

(b) Anywhere in the range 83–85.[1]

Agility

Agility is the ability to move and change the direction of your body quickly whilst maintaining control.

Rugby players need agility to sidestep around opposing players to avoid a tackle and gain territory.

Illinois agility run test

This test measures agility. It requires **eight cones**, carefully arranged at measured distances apart as shown in the diagram.

The performer starts face down and runs against a **stopwatch timer** to the end. The activity is measured in seconds.

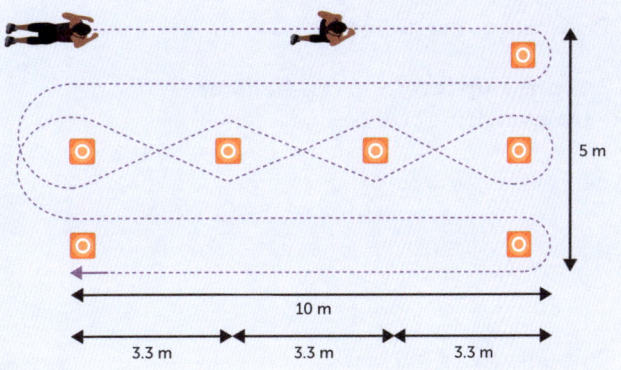

2. Speed and agility are useful in sports that require sudden changes of direction, such as football and badminton. The table below shows some test results for a group of male <18 football players.

Performer	30 metre (seconds)	Illinois agility test (seconds)
Joe	4.2	15.8
Karl	4.6	16.4
Mason	4.3	16.3

(a) Which player appears to be slowest? [1]
(b) Which player has the greatest agility? [1]

(a) Karl[1]   (b) Joe[1]

 ## Strength

Strength is the ability to overcome a resistance. It can be further categorised as maximal, static, dynamic and explosive strength. Strength can be measured using the grip strength dynamometer test.

High maximal strength is required in **boxing** and **weightlifting**. Static strength helps **rugby players** to hold the resistance in a scrum position. **Gymnasts** have high dynamic strength.

Grip strength dynamometer test

This measures grip strength. Using a handgrip dynamometer in the dominant hand, squeeze the handle with maximum effort keeping the elbow at 90 degrees. Record the best score.

Muscular endurance

Muscular endurance is the ability of a muscle or muscle group to undergo repeated contractions, without fatigue. It can be measured using the press-up test or the sit-up test.

Triathletes require muscular endurance for **running**, **swimming** and **cycling** to reduce fatigue in muscles repeatedly contracting. **Canoeists** and **football players** also benefit.

One-minute press-up test

The **press-up test** requires a **flat area** and a **stopwatch**. Using the correct technique, participants start with their arms extended and perform as many press-ups in a minute as they can. Resting is permitted only in the raised position. Performance is measured according to age and gender.

One-minute sit-up test

The **sit-up test** requires a partner to support the feet and ankles, and to press play on an audio recording of progressively faster bleeps. The participant sits up and back down again to the rhythm of the bleeps.

As a **maximal test**, the sit ups continue until the participant can no longer keep time with the bleeps. The score is equal to the number of sit ups performed.

3. Evaluate the use of the press up test for a sprint cyclist. [2]

   3. The test measures the muscular endurance of the upper body and arms only.[1] Sprint cyclists need muscular endurance[1] but they rely on their leg muscles which are not tested using this method.[1]

Speed

Speed is the ability to move body parts to perform an action quickly. It can be measured using the 30m sprint test.

Sprinters and **tennis players** require speed to move quickly across a track or court.

30m sprint test

4. The 30 metre sprint test measures speed. Describe how to carry out this test. [3]

4. Use 2 cones[1] and place them 30 metres apart using a tape measure.[1] Allow a flying start to the sprint[1] and with a stop watch, time the athlete running as they pass between the start and end cones.[1] Record the time in seconds.[1]

 Power

Power (or **explosive strength**) is the product of strength and speed, i.e. strength × speed. Power can be measured using the standing or vertical jump test.

Power is crucial in **sprint sports**, **boxing**, **shot put** and **volleyball** to provide bursts of power when needed. For example, to get out of the blocks first, create a final burst to the finish line, put a shot or smash a ball with strength and speed.

Vertical jump test

The **vertical jump test** involves a **wall**, a **ruler** or **measuring tape**, and some **chalk** to make a mark with. With flat feet, stand and reach up the wall as high as possible and record the height.

Now, jump as high as possible using your arms and legs and make a mark using chalked hands or ask an assistant to record the height. Measure the distance between the standing reach height and the jump height in centimetres.

5. Discuss the suitability of the vertical jump test for measuring the explosive power of a javelin thrower. [5]

   5. The vertical jump test largely measures the power of the legs, whereas a javelin thrower's power needs to come predominately from the arm and shoulder.[1] A javelin thrower needs a more muscular physique, adding bodyweight which would be harder to lift in a vertical jump.[1] Jumping does not replicate the movements of javelin throwing so would not be so useful as a performance measure.[1] As a maximal test, it can help to motivate and push performance.[1] Legs are involved in javelin throwing, so measuring their strength is helpful.[1]

Flexibility

Flexibility is a measure of the range of movements possible at a joint. It can be measured using the 'sit and reach' test.

Gymnasts, **divers**, **martial artists** and **figure skaters** require excellent flexibility to increase their range of movement and to reduce injury.

Sit and reach test

Using a **sit and reach box**, the athlete sits on the floor with their bare feet flat against the box and their legs straight. The athlete then reaches forwards as far as possible to move the slider. The slider records how far in centimetres they are from zero (their feet).

6. Give **two** reasons why a participant may not perform well on the sit and reach test. [2]

   6. Two from: Tight hamstrings / short inelastic muscles / did not stretch or warm up,[1] injured,[1] related muscle groups are rarely used,[1] short arms and long legs,[1] males are generally less flexible,[1] the test may be measured or performed incorrectly,[1] lack of motivation to try.[1]

THE PRINCIPLES OF TRAINING

Key principles of training

The key principles of training are provided as guidance when designing a training programme. Following the principles of training will help to make training effective.

Individual needs

A **personal exercise plan** (**PEP**) should be created to suit the needs, age, gender and abilities of the individual so that it is of the right level of demand and considers any injuries.

Specificity

Training programmes should be specific to the sport, in terms of training goals, movements, muscles used, intensity and energy systems. For example, to build specific muscle groups identified as needing improvement, or developing specific skills related to an athlete's sport, e.g. free or penalty kicks in field sports.

Progressive overload

Progress means to gradually increase the intensity of training so that fitness gains occur. Progress should be gradual in order to avoid injury. Overload is required to push your body beyond its comfortable limits to provide challenge, overcome plateaus in development and drive progress. Working harder than normal and putting your body under stress will result in adaptations and improvements to your body.

Overtraining

Exercising too hard and too often can limit the body's opportunity to rest and recover. This will start to reverse the benefits of training and could cause injury.

Reversibility

Reversibility states that athletes will undo their progress if their training schedule lapses or becomes less demanding. Fitness gains and skill levels may decrease.

> Time out through injury is the most common cause of reversibility.

The elements of FITT

The elements of FITT are useful in optimising a training plan in order to achieve fitness goals. FITT can also be used to apply the principle of overload.

F Frequency

How often do training sessions happen? Two or three times a week is considered a good start but this may increase as required.

I Intensity

How hard are the training sessions? Weights may be increased, resistance on a rowing machine may be increased or an incline may be introduced for runners.

T Time

How long do sessions last for? As fitness increases, sessions, reps or sets may increase. Rest periods may also decrease.

T Type

What type of training is done in each session? Switching between types of training (**pages 45–49**) adds variety, helps with overload, provides different fitness benefits and prevents boredom.

Samira is training for a basketball match. Explain how Samira can use the training principle of specificity to improve her performance in the game. [2]

Work on the muscles / movement / energy systems used in basketball.[1] Work on agility with a ball to replicate the movements and intensity in a game.[1] Increase standing jump performance by working on the legs.[1] Practice set pieces or drills.[1]

THRESHOLDS OF TRAINING

The **training threshold** is defined as the level of intensity required to produce an improvement in performance or adaptation of the body to better suit the sport.

Calculating the aerobic and anaerobic training zone

The simplified **Karvonen formula** is used to calculate the correct training zone for a performer. For training to be most effective, the athlete must remain in the right target zone for their own fitness aims:

Maximum heart rate =	220 (Beats Per Minute) − Age
Aerobic training zone:	60% − 80% of maximal heart rate
Anaerobic training zone:	80% − 90% of maximal heart rate

Worked example:

Abi is a 20 year old swimmer calculating her anaerobic training zone:

220 − 20 = 200 BPM Maximum heart rate

200 × 0.8 = 160 BPM Upper training threshold at 80% of MaxHR

200 × 0.9 = 180 BPM Lower training threshold at 90% of MaxHR

Abi should adapt her training so that her heart remains in the 160–180 BPM range in order to achieve maximum anaerobic benefit.

Romy is a 30 year old lacrosse player. She is looking to increase the effectiveness of her circuit training by remaining in the aerobic zone.

(a) Calculate the upper and lower threshold of her aerobic target zone. [2]

Romy's percentage maximum heart rate values were monitored during every two minutes during training. These are shown in **Figure 1**.

Figure 1

(b) State how many minutes that Romy remained within her aerobic target zone. [1]

(a) 220 − 30 = 190 BPM Maximum heart rate
190 × 0.8 = 152[1] BPM Upper training threshold at 80% of MaxHR
190 × 0.6 = 114[1] BPM Lower training threshold at 60% of MaxHR
(b) 20 minutes.[1] From 6 to 26 minutes.

3.2.5 **3.3.2** **3.3.3**

TYPES OF TRAINING

There are many different types of training, each with their own distinctions. Varying the type of training used helps to reduce boredom, increase commitment to fitness and avoids injury through repetitive strain.

> Any training and practice method must take account of the purpose, the effects on the body and the recovery.

Continuous training

Continuous training involves sustained exercise at a **constant rate** (or **steady state**) with **no rest**. It involves **aerobic demand** for a minimum of 20 minutes, for example running, swimming, rowing or cycling.

> Athletes and coaches should consider their fitness or sport requirements, the facilities available and their current level of fitness when deciding on the most appropriate training methods and intensities.

Advantages
- Improves cardiovascular and muscular endurance.
- Increases muscular strength in active muscles.
- Less intense on joints compared with other training methods.
- Can change body shape over time to become an ectomorph / more streamlined.

Disadvantages
- Continuous movements may result in injury from repetitive contractions.
- May not increase power as it is not anaerobic.
- Can result in tedium / boredom.
- Longer training sessions can take a lot of time.

---

1. George is training for a marathon. He has chosen to use continuous training. Discuss whether continuous training is an effective training method for George. [6]

   1. Continuous training is sustained for at least 20 minutes at a constant pace. (AO1)[✓] It is a form of training that has a relatively low impact on his joints and ligaments. (AO2)[✓] This can help George to avoid injury. (AO3)[✓] Continuous training by running can closely replicate the movements of a marathon (AO2)[✓] and requires no specialist equipment. (AO1)[✓] He is likely to improve his cardiovascular / aerobic endurance and may improve his body shape (AO2),[✓] reducing his weight (AO3)[✓] and increasing speed. (AO3)[✓] Continuous training is suitable for individuals (AO1) as programmes need to be tailored which may suit George (AO2)[✓] as he needs to follow a training programme that is suitable for his own level of fitness, challenge and experience. (AO3)[✓]

      George may become bored (AO2)[✓] by running constantly so could vary exercise with cycling or swimming. (AO3)[✓] However, this would not replicate the movements of a marathon so closely. (AO3)[✓] George could supplement his training (AO2)[✓] with other techniques such as interval training and static stretching to increase strength and lengthen his stride / range of motion which would improve his performance. (AO3)[✓]

   This question should be marked in accordance with the levels-based mark scheme on page 123.

Fartlek training

Fartlek is the Swedish term for 'speed play'. This involves **varying the speed**, **terrain** and **work:recovery ratios** of exercises. It is related to continuous training and interval training. Intensity is varied over different terrain, gradients or speed of activity.

Advantages

- Improves speed, cardiovascular and muscular endurance.
- Combines aerobic and anaerobic activity.
- Helps with pace and an awareness of your physical response to changes in intensity.

Disadvantages

- Needs to be tailored to the individual so unsuitable for groups.
- Requires discipline to continuously undertake unstructured exercise.
- Experience is required to ensure that training is at the right level of intensity.

---

2. Jo plays competitive rugby and is looking to improve her performance. Evaluate the appropriateness of Fartlek training for Jo. [6]

2. AO1: Fartlek training is known as speed play.[✓] It generally involves running and changing the speed and terrain at different points in the run.[✓]

AO2 and AO3: Fartlek training is ideal for game sports that consist of short bursts of anaerobic sprinting mixed with aerobic recovery periods (AO2)[✓] as it helps the body to cope with varying intensities of match play. (AO3)[✓] It helps to develop the use of power and explosive strength (AO2)[✓] which are needed during fast game play such as a sprint to the try line. (AO3)[✓] Lower intensity training improves cardiovascular / aerobic endurance (AO2)[✓] which is necessary to get through a match without tiring at the end. (AO3)[✓] Mind/body awareness can also be improved (AO2)[✓] which helps Jo understand how her body may react to sudden changes in the demand she puts on it. (AO3)[✓] Jo may not be able to train using Fartlek with the whole team as the programme needs to be tailored to the individual which will differ according to their goals or player position. (AO3)[✓] This may reduce the opportunity for team bonding (AO3)[✓] and doesn't replicate true match conditions or gameplay. (AO3)[✓] Training may improve power (AO2)[✓] which will assist Jo with scrums, sprints and tackles. (AO3)[✓] Since Fartlek is often used during the playing season, injury during training may mean that she misses future fixtures. (AO3)[✓] Jo can use the principles of training and FITT. (AO2)[✓] Jo may combine her training with weight training, HIIT training or plyometrics (AO2) to improve all-round power and strength. (AO3)[✓]

This question should be marked in accordance with the levels-based mark scheme on page 123.

Circuit training

Circuit training involves roughly 6–12 **stations**, each with a different exercise designed to achieve the aims of the participants. Station activities will depend on the **space** and **equipment** available. The demand of a circuit can be altered according to the exercise or by changing the **work:rest ratio** to decrease rest and achieve overload more quickly.

Advantages

- Can be used by large groups.
- Easy to set up.
- Usually involves little equipment so it is inexpensive to organise.
- Content or demand can be widely adapted to suit most training goals / components of fitness.
- Can be tailored to train the whole body or specific parts of it.
- Different intensities can be programmed to train aerobically and anaerobically.
- Exercises can replicate specific sporting movements

Disadvantages

- Isolated exercises may not always be totally sport specific.
- Does not replicate 'real time' match play situations or competition.
- Technique can be affected by muscle fatigue which can increase the risk of injury.

3. The type of training should be adapted to ensure that the heart and body are working at the right level to achieve the fitness aims of the individual.

   (a) Other than rest, give **one** way in which circuit training can be altered to determine the fitness aim. [2]
   (b) State what is meant by the work:rest ratio. [1]

   (a) Two from: Time[1], content.[1]
   (b) The period of time spent exercising at a station compared to the period of rest in between stations.[1]

Interval training

Interval training involves periods of exercising hard, interspersed with periods of rest or low intensity exercise. **High intensity interval training** (**HIIT**) increases the level of demand over standard interval training and involves more active rest. It involves the repetition of short bursts of anaerobic activity with rest periods in between.

Advantages

- Develops aerobic and anaerobic fitness.
- Easily adapted for specific outcomes and fitness components.

Disadvantages

- Can be very tiring which requires discipline and motivation.
- Intensity can cause injury if not properly managed.

4. Matt is a hockey player.
   Explain how interval training could be used to improve Matt's hockey performance. [2]

4. Training would use sprints / anaerobic bursts[1] interspersed with rests[1] which would mimic the demands / be specific to hockey[1] as performance is at different intensities.[1]
   Hockey involves short bursts of high intensity movement / action[1] followed by active rest in slower parts of the game.[1]

Plyometric training

Plyometric training involves **hopping**, **bounding** or **jumping** to develop **power**, **speed** and **explosive strength**. Plyometrics makes use of gravity to extend muscles (eccentric contraction) before making a larger concentric contraction. For example, jumping off a box into a deep squat to lengthen the quadriceps before jumping higher onto another box.

Advantages

- Simulates many sporting movements such as those in high jump, volleyball, sprint starts and javelin throwing.
- No specialist equipment required.

Disadvantages

- Requires a high level of fitness to start with as there is a high risk of injury.
- Repetitive jumping and bounding can cause stress on the joints.

Weight or resistance training

Weight training or **resistance training** involves lifting weights using different muscle groups to develop **strength** and **muscular endurance**. The choice of weight or exercise depends on the fitness aim. Weights may include free weights, medicine balls or resistance machines. A safe lifting technique, using a straight back, is necessary to reduce injury. A spotter may also be required to ensure safety with free weights.

Advantages
- Exercises and reps are easily adapted for specific muscular strength or endurance.
- Can be done by anyone, using anything with resistance.

Disadvantages
- Poor technique and lifting too much can cause injury.
- Muscle ache a day or so after training is common.

---

5. Erik is a weight lifter.
   Explain how Erik can use weight training to improve maximal strength in his quadriceps. [2]

   Weights of almost the maximum weight that Erik can lift should be lifted a very low number of repetitions before resting.[1] He should repeat this for a few sets[1] with a short period of rest in between.[1]

| 3.2.5 | 3.3.2 | 3.3.3 |

FITNESS CLASSES

A variety of fitness classes are available to improve specific components of fitness, physical activity and sport.

Body pump

Body pump is a group fitness class involving high repetition actions such as squats, curls and lunges with the use of low weights to add resistance.

Core fitness components: Cardiovascular fitness, body composition, muscular endurance and strength.

Aerobics

Aerobics involves exercising to music, combining a variety of movements and actions.

Core fitness components: Cardiovascular fitness and flexibility.

Pilates

Pilates focuses on building strength and stability through repetitive resistance exercises. It commonly involves the use of mats, resistance bands and other specialist equipment.

Core fitness components: Muscular endurance, flexibility and core strength.

Yoga

Yoga is a physical, mental and spiritual practice using floor mats upon which participants hold different postures and perform breathing exercises. This can have a positive impact on health and well-being as well as fitness.

Core fitness components: Muscular endurance, flexibility, balance and core strength.

Spinning

Spinning classes use exercise bikes, commonly with music and a group instructor to motivate participants.

Core fitness components: Cardiovascular fitness, muscular endurance, body composition.

THE LONG-TERM EFFECTS OF EXERCISE ON THE MUSCULAR-SKELETAL SYSTEM

The long-term effects of exercise can make gradual, but significant improvements in specific **components of fitness** (see **pages 36** to **37**). The exact benefits of exercise depend on the type of activities that are undertaken.

Long-term effects and benefits

Increased bone density

Bone density increases as muscles pull on them creating more work for them, building their strength and thickness. This increases the protection of a performer's skeletal system and internal organs in contact sports. It also helps to reduce **osteoporosis**.

Increased strength of ligaments and tendons

Strength increases through repeated resistance exercises. This can reduce the chance of injury through other training activities or competitive sports.

Increased muscular endurance

Muscular endurance helps you perform stronger and for longer. The ability to move your body and muscles repeatedly without fatiguing increases with regular exercise. This is especially helpful for endurance athletes and games players.

Greater resistance to fatigue

Muscles become less tired through greater efficiency of the body to produce energy.

Hypertrophy is the name given to the enlargement of skeletal or cardiac muscle through micro-tears that heal, increasing mass.

Muscle hypertrophy

Skeletal muscles will increase in size as a result of training or exercise over a sustained period of time. This could provide a competitive advantage over a smaller performer.

Greater muscular strength

Larger muscles can increase power and explosive strength in a rugby game for example.

The importance of rest

Rest is necessary for adaptations to take place and for the body to recover before the next training session.

| 3.4.1 | 3.4.2 | 3.4.4 | 1.4.5 |

THE LONG-TERM EFFECTS OF EXERCISE ON THE CARDIO-RESPIRATORY SYSTEM

A long-term exercise programme enables performers to train for longer and more intensely.

Long-term effects and benefits

Decreased resting heart rate (bradycardia) occurs as a healthier, more muscular, heart can achieve a **higher stroke volume**, delivering sufficient oxygen to a resting body with fewer beats and therefore with greater efficiency.

Increased capillarisation is an increase in the number of capillaries as a result of regular exercise over time. The density of capillaries around the alveoli and surrounding muscles increases to facilitate more efficient gas exchange.

Drop in resting blood pressure happens as a result of a more elastic muscular wall of veins and arteries.

Improved rate of recovery enables a performer to be ready for the next match, event or training more quickly. Lactic acid can also be removed more effectively through increased cardiac output.

Increased lung capacity and vital capacity develops as stronger lungs and heart muscles are able to deliver oxygen to the working muscles more efficiently so a performer can work harder and for longer without tiring.

Increased resting stroke volume and **maximum cardiac output** occurs as a stronger heart results in a thicker wall of the left ventricle which can pump out more blood with **stronger contractions**.

Increased size and strength of the heart (cardiac hypertrophy) results in a stronger, healthier heart reducing the resting heart rate and the risk of heart attacks, angina and coronory heart disease.

Increased number of red blood cells facilitates greater oxygen transport to the working muscles, increasing the aerobic intensity they are able to work at.

Increased number of alveoli occurs as the lungs increase in size. The surface area of the alveoli also increases, making gas exchange more efficient.

Increased strength of diaphragm and external intercostal muscles through hypertrophy improves breathing and tidal volume.

1. Explain why cardiac hypertrophy can result in a lower resting heart rate. [2]
2. Paul plays hockey and has tested his fitness in each month of training over a one year period. His results are shown in the graph below.

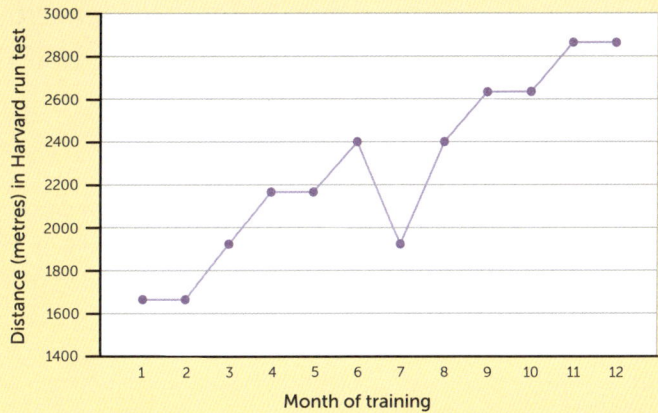

(a) Discuss how the long term effects of exercise on cardiovascular endurance and aerobic power could be beneficial to Paul. [3]
(b) Give **one** reason why month 7 may have been lower than expected. [1]

1. Cardiac hypertrophy is an increase in the size of the heart[1] which means that stroke volume can increase / more blood is ejected per beat.[1] Increasing the size of the heart[1] means that it can pump an increased volume of blood around the body with each cycle.[1] As the body size remains the same, the heart no longer needs to work as hard to deliver sufficient blood to the organs at rest[1] so the heart rate lowers.[1]

2. (a) Increase in endurance means that Paul is able to perform for a whole match without tiring.[1]
    Increased rate of removal of lactic acid means that Paul can play harder for longer.[1]
    A greater resistance to fatigue so Paul can play for longer or play harder.[1]
    Stronger respiratory muscles help Paul to deliver more oxygen to the working muscles.[1]
    Hypertrophy of the heart means that Paul may be able to play hockey for more years and reduce his risk of related diseases.[1]

   (b) Reversibility,[1] off day,[1] illness,[1] injury,[1] test taken too soon after a match, so insufficient recovery time.[1]

3.5.1

PARQ ASSESSMENTS

PARQ stands for **Physical Activity Readiness Questionnaire**. A PARQ assessment is a short questionnaire to help trainers, coaches or fitness centre staff to determine any risks or safety considerations for an individual based on their health and medical history.

PARQ

PARQ assessments are carried out before an individual begins any kind of fitness work in order:

- To review medical history
- To determine any potential heart conditions that may make training unsafe
- To assess readiness for safe exercise
- To make recommendations for amendments to training or personal exercise programme (PEP) based on any health issues.

> Give **one** example of someone who may ask people for a PARQ assessment. [2]
>
> *Answers include: Teacher responsible for students using a weights room.*[1] *Fitness instructor working in a gym.*[1] *Personal trainer.*[1] *Performance coach.*[1]

> **! Note**
>
> You will need to carry out a PARQ assessment as part of your Personal Exercise Plan assessment. See **page 115**.

PARQ Health Questionnaire

Please read the questions carefully and answer honestly by ticking the appropriate box and/or adding information if necessary. Your response will be kept in strict confidence.

This form must be completed and returned to your Fitness Advisor and assessed prior to any induction.

Name:

Have you ever been diagnosed with a heart problem? Y N

In the past month have you had any chest pain when:
Doing an activity Y N   You were resting Y N

Are you taking any medication for:
A heart condition Y N   Any other problems Y N

Do you suffer from any bone and/or joint problems? Y N

In the past year have you had any major illnesses or surgery? Y N

Have you ever been diagnosed with:
Diabetes Y N   Epilepsy Y N   Other problems Y N
Asthma Y N

Are you pregnant? Y N   Recently had a baby? Y N
If you've recently had a baby, how long ago was the birth?

Do you ever lose your balance or consciousness? Y N

Are you currently feeling unwell? (E.g. due to a cold.) Y N

If you have answered YES to one or more of the questions above, we may need to contact your doctor before starting an exercise plan.
If any of your responses change to a YES, please tell your Fitness Advisor as soon as possible.

I have read, understood and completed this questionnaire to the best of my knowledge. Any questions I had were answered satisfactorily by my Fitness Advisor.

Signed: Date:

INJURY PREVENTION

3.5.2

In order to prevent injury, risks can be minimised by using appropriate clothing, equipment, correct lifting techniques, using a warm up and cool down and an appropriate level of competition.

Factors in the prevention of injury

Correct clothing and footwear
Clothing and accessories should be appropriately sized, tied and attached. Loose clothing can cause entanglement. Loose laces could cause tripping, jewellery should be removed where applicable and hair should be tied back.

Correct footwear helps to prevent blisters, provides toe protection, ankle support and cushioning. Studs or spikes in footwear can be worn to reduce slipping.

Personal protective equipment
Protective equipment, for example, a scrum cap, helmet, shin pads, gloves or gum shields can protect against injury and allow safe movement.

Correct application of the principles of training
Overuse injuries can be reduced by using **progressive overload** to **gradually** increase training intensity. **Rest and recovery** periods should be appropriate to allow the body to recover and repair between training sessions.

Checking equipment and facilities
Damaged or inappropriate equipment or facilities can cause injury. Consider the impact of, for example, a broken safety cord on a running machine, improperly secured weights on a barbell, damaged benches for weight or circuit training, spillages, tears to Astro pitch surfaces or broken glass on a playing field.

Correct application and adherence to the rules
Sports rules are often there for safety, for example lifting a hockey stick above head height or hitting below the belt in boxing.

---

1. Give **two** ways in which performers are grouped according to sports rules to avoid injury. Suggest a relevant sport for each. [4]

2. A class of students is taken to a local sports centre for a hockey match on an Astro pitch. State **two** safety checks that the teacher in charge should carry out on the facilities before the match commences. [2]

---

1. Performers are often separated by age group (youth athletics),[1] experience/skill level (skiing),[1] weight (boxing),[1] ranking (judo)[1] or gender (sprinting)[1] to help match like for like performers against each other.[1] Accept any suitable sporting activities.

2. Checks may include: ensure there are no wrinkled, bald, or damaged surface areas that could cause tripping or other injury.[1] Inadequate water or sand applied.[1] Poorly maintained or damaged equipment.[1] Insufficient run-out space from boundary or equipment stores.[1] Poor lighting if played after dark.[1] Litter and debris, including cans, glass or stones.[1]

INJURIES THAT CAN OCCUR IN PHYSICAL ACTIVITY AND SPORT

Common injuries

Concussion

Concussion can occur as a result of an impact to the head. This is likely in contact sports such as rugby, through heading a ball in football or in individual sports such as diving, where a diver may hit their head on the diving board or the surface of the water with a bad entry.

Dislocation

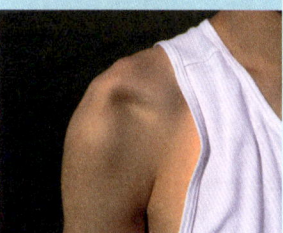

Dislocations are injuries in joints causing bones to separate from their sockets. It is possible to dislocate most joints, but shoulder dislocations are the most common, usually associated with a fall or blow in sports such as gymnastics, skiing or volleyball.

Sprain

A **sprain** is a torn muscle or **ligament**. Overuse, overstretching or force from a knock or fall can cause a sprain which results in inflammation. Sprained ankles are common in many sports, especially in ball sports and track and field where athletes may land awkwardly.

Sprains and strains can be caused by overstretching or twisting a muscle. Not warming up before exercising or playing sport, and tired muscles are common causes.

Fractures

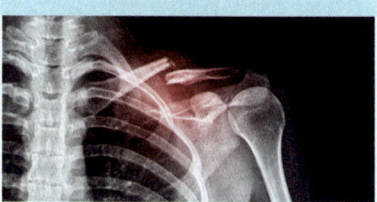

Fractures are a break or partial break in a bone. They can occur as a result of falling, contact with a stationary object or contact with a moving object or person. High speed or contact sports such as mountain biking, skiing or lacrosse commonly result in breaks in the hand, wrist, ribs and collar bones (as shown).

Stress fractures are very fine cracks in a bone caused by overuse, typically in the feet of runners.

Soft tissue injury

Soft tissue injury includes **strain**, **tennis elbow**, **golfers' elbow** and **abrasions** (**grazes**). A strain is a twist, pull, or tear of a muscle or tendon. Repetitive movements such as tennis serves or golf swings can cause strains at the elbow. Grazes tend to occur as a result of impact injuries at speed, for example, falling off a bicycle.

Torn cartilage

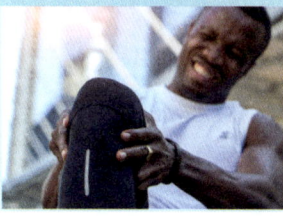

Torn cartilage can occur as a result of direct force or twisting – commonly to the knee. In older performers, it may happen as the result of years of wear and tear. Torn knee cartilage can cause pain, swelling and restricted movement.

3.5.4

RICE

RICE is an acronym for **rest**, **ice**, **compression** and **elevation**. It is common first aid practice for treating **sprains** and **strains** to reduce pain and swelling. This maintains blood flow to the injured site to speed up recovery.

Practice advice

R Rest

Stop any exercise or activity, avoid excessive movement and try not to put any weight on the injury.

I Ice

Apply an ice pack to the injury for up to 20 minutes every 2 to 3 hours.

A bag of snow, frozen peas or sweetcorn wrapped in a thin cloth can work equally well as an ice pack.

C Compression

Gently wrap a bandage around the injury to provide support and reduce pain.

E Elevation

Keep the injury raised, ideally above the heart, as much as possible to reduce swelling. A pillow can be used for support.

Give **one** sporting example of an injury that would require first aid treatment using the RICE principles. [1]

Answers may include: A sprained ankle caused by a bad landing in the 110m hurdles.[1] A strained muscle or tendon aggravated by repetitive golf swings.[1]

Edexcel GCSE **Physical Education – Paper 1, Topic 3**

3.5.5

PERFORMANCE-ENHANCING DRUGS (PEDs)

Performance-enhancing drugs (PEDs) are substances that are designed to improve performance. They are often prohibited (banned) and when taken, break the contract to compete.

> Remember that drugs can be addictive (as a negative side-effect).

Anabolic steroids
Sprinting, weightlifting, boxing

- ⊕ Increases rate and amount of muscle growth
- ⊕ Increases power and strength
- ⊕ Allows you to train harder for longer
- ⊕ Speeds up recovery so more training can be done
- ⊕ Increases aggression and competitiveness.

- ⊖ Causes a hormonal imbalance
- ⊖ Raises blood pressure
- ⊖ Damages the liver, kidneys and heart.

Stimulants
Power sports, combat sports

- ⊕ Increases alertness
- ⊕ Reduces tiredness
- ⊕ Increases aggression
- ⊕ Speeds up parts of the body, for example a 100m sprinter will react and move more quickly out of the blocks.

- ⊖ Causes high blood pressure
- ⊖ Increases chance of strokes, heart and liver problems
- ⊖ Increases the likelihood of performing with an injury.

Beta-blockers
Archery, diving, shooting

- ⊕ Reduces anxiety
- ⊕ Reduces muscle tremors and shaking, improving precision
- ⊕ Reduces heart rate.

- ⊖ Slows the heart rate reducing oxygen to the brain and muscles
- ⊖ Fatigue and drowsiness.

Narcotic analgesics
Martial arts, general sports

- ⊕ Masks pain or injury to continue performing.

- ⊖ Lowers blood pressure
- ⊖ Lowers concentration, leading to coma
- ⊖ Causes constipation
- ⊖ Creates a temptation to compete whilst injured.

Blood doping
Marathon running, distance cycling, triathlon

- ⊕ Increases red blood cell count
- ⊕ Increases oxygen delivery to the muscles
- ⊕ Can work aerobically for longer.

Diuretics
Boxing, horse riding, martial arts

- ⊕ Causes rapid weight loss
- ⊕ Dilutes the presence of illegal substances
- ⊕ Removes excessive fluid.

- ⊖ Causes dehydration
- ⊖ Lowers blood pressure
- ⊖ Causes muscle cramps.

Peptide hormones (Erythropoietin – EPO) (Growth hormones – GH)
Distance athletes

- ⊕ Increases red blood cells
- ⊕ Increases oxygen delivery to the muscles
- ⊕ Can work aerobically for longer
- ⊕ Increases muscle growth.

- ⊖ Increases the viscosity (thickening) of the blood
- ⊖ Increases stress on the heart
- ⊖ Increases the risk of stroke.

- ⊖ Thickens the blood
- ⊖ Potential infection
- ⊖ Danger of an embolism (blockage of a blood vessel)
- ⊖ Potential for heart attack

1. Give **one** visible effect of taking anabolic agents. [1]

   1. *Positive effect: increased muscle mass.[1] Negative effect (caused by a hormonal imbalance): shrinking testicles / deeper female voice / increased female body hair / smaller breasts.[1]*

You are required to know the name, positive effects and negative side-effects of each type of PED.

You do not need to learn examples of each PED type.

The process of blood doping

Blood doping involves the use of techniques or substances to increase a performer's red blood cell (RBC) count.

| 1 | Blood is removed from an athlete several weeks before competition. |

| 2 | The blood is frozen. |

| 3 | The body makes more red blood cells to replace the ones that have been removed. |

| 4 | 1–2 days before competition, the frozen blood is thawed and injected back into the performer, thus increasing their red blood cell count. |

| 5 | The performer now has more red blood cells which increases their oxygen carrying capacity and aerobic performance. |

> **! Note**
>
> Caution! Blood doping comes with many negative side effects: thickening of the blood (viscosity), potential infection, potential for heart attack, and an embolism (blockage of a blood vessel).

2. Suggest which component of fitness is improved by using the prohibited method of blood doping.

   Justify your answer with a sporting example. [4]

   2. *Cardiovascular endurance.[1] Example: long-distance athletes.[1] Justification: Any two from: to increase red blood cell count[1] so their oxygen carrying capacity in the blood in increased.[1] Improves the efficiency of the aerobic system.[1] Maintains performance without suffering from fatigue / excess lactic acid.[1]*

Edexcel GCSE **Physical Education – Paper 1, Topic 3**

TYPES OF PERFORMERS THAT MAY USE DIFFERENT TYPES OF PEDs

Stimulants

Increase alertness.

A **sprinter** may take stimulants to be alert in the blocks.

Anabolic agents

Increase muscle mass.

Any athlete requiring power and strength may take anabolic steroids e.g., a **discus thrower**.

Peptide hormones (EPO)

Increase oxygen carrying capacity.

Road cyclists may take peptide hormones to improve aerobic performance.

Blood doping

Increases oxygen carrying capacity.

Endurance athletes have been known to use blood doping to enhance the efficiency of their aerobic system.

Beta-blockers

Increase fine motor control.

Archers may take beta blockers to enhance concentration and precision.

Diuretics

For weight loss.

Boxers or **jockeys** may take diuretics to make a weight category.

Narcotic analgesics

Relieve pain from over-training.

Narcotic analgesics allow injured athletes in **any sport** to continue training or competing.

Using a different sporting example for each, justify why one performer may take diuretics and another performer beta blockers. [4]

Diuretics for a martial artist[1] to make a weight category / sprinter to flush out other illegal drugs they may have taken (or equivalent).[1] Beta blockers by a shooter[1] to gain an unfair advantage by increasing precision, accuracy and concentration (or equivalent).[1]

3.6.1

THE PURPOSE AND IMPORTANCE OF WARM-UPS AND COOL DOWNS

Warming up and cooling down routines significantly increase an athlete's ability to train to a higher level, to train more frequently, to avoid injury and to achieve better results.

Warming up

Stretching the muscles increases pliability and flexibility, reducing the risk of injury. Sports related skills and drills are also commonly included.

This increases the amount of oxygen to the working muscles and provides mental preparation so that the athlete is ready for the main training session or competition.

Benefits of warming up include:
- The warming effect on body temperature
- Increased range of movement by warming the muscles to make them more elastic
- A gradual increase of effort to full pace to avoid physical or mental shock
- Psychological preparation
- The practice of physical skills through the whole range of movement
- Steps to reduce and prevent injury.

Cooling down

Cooling down requires maintaining an elevated breathing and heart rate by including a walk or jog, for example. Stretching allows muscles to lengthen whilst warm and then relax. A gradual reduction in intensity prevents overheating, light-headedness and nausea.

It also provides an opportunity to increase **excess post-exercise oxygen consumption** (**EPOC**) to repay the **oxygen debt** and encourages blood flow to return to the inactive organs and away from active muscles to prevent **blood pooling**.

Benefits of cooling down include:
- Allowing the body to recover
- To gradually reduce heart rate to aid removal of lactic acid, CO_2 and waste products
- To reduce (delayed onset) muscle soreness (DOMS).

Explain why it is important to warm up before an intensive training session. [3]

Three from: Gradually increase heart rate in preparation for exercise.[1] Gradually increase blood flow around the body to warm muscles.[1] Stretch and lengthen muscles to increase range of motion to prevent injury before stress.[1] Increase oxygen flow to the working muscles in preparation for exercise.[1] Prepare the mind for intense exercise and focus on training.[1] Encourage blood flow to divert from the inactive organs to the active muscles.[1]

PHASES AND ACTIVITIES OF WARM-UPS AND COOL DOWNS

Warming up routines have three phases of light to moderate exercise. Cool down activities should include moderate, but not intense exercise, similar to those used for warm-ups.

Warming up activities

Warming up should include an activity that gradually raises the pulse, readying the heart and muscles for exercise.

Phases of a warm up

1 Pulse raising

- Warms up muscles and prepares the body for physical activity
- Increases oxygen delivery to the working muscles
- Raises body temperature slowly
- Gradually raises heart rate up to full pace to avoid physical or mental shock.

2 Stretching, mobility and dynamic movements

Mobility takes joints through their full range of movement in order to loosen them, for example shoulder rotations, lunges and lateral rotations of the neck. **Dynamic movements** involve speed or changes of direction.

- Improves the flexibility of muscles and joints
- Improves the pliability of ligaments and tendons
- Increases muscle temperature and range of movement
- Increases the speed of muscle contraction.

3 Skills practice and drills

- Aids psychological preparation and confidence
- Accesses muscle memory
- Practices core or common skills used in a game, for example, a tennis player may practice serves, volleys, back hands and forehand shots.

Cooling down activities

Cardiovascular activities such as **walking** or **jogging** help to maintain an elevated breathing rate after exercise and should help to gradually reduce the intensity of the main activity. Low intensity **stretching** will also help muscles to lengthen after the intense contractions of exercise. Lastly, performers should **rehydrate** and **refuel** to replace lost fluids and energy.

1. Dynamic movements are a key component of a warm up.

   Describe **two** different practical examples of dynamic exercises which could be used as part of a warm up for a named sporting activity. [1]

2. Ronny plays football for his local team.

   (a) Give **one** way that Ronny could cool down after a match. [1]

   (b) Other than a cool down, describe how Ronny could aide his recovery after an intense match. [2]

---

1. Shuttle runs would be helpful to a football player / tennis player to help them increase their speed and agility.[1] Skipping helps to increase speed for a boxer.[1] Zig-zagging around cones helps rugby players with side stepping.[1] High knee kicks would help a footballer or high jumper to warm up and stretch the hamstrings.[1]

2. (a) Stretching,[1] gentle jog / low intensity movements.[1]

   (b) Answers may include: Drink plenty of water to rehydrate,[1] replacing water[1] and minerals lost through sweat. Take an ice bath[1] to reduce muscle soreness.[1] Eat simple carbohydrates[1] to replenish glycogen stores.[1]

Edexcel GCSE **Physical Education** – Paper 1, Topic 3

Paper 1, Topic 3

EXAMINATION PRACTICE

1. Which **one** of the following is not a component of fitness? [1]
   - ☐ A – Agility
   - ☐ B – Balance
   - ☐ C – Coordination
   - ☐ D – Decision making

2. In which of these sporting activities is reaction time most important? [1]
   - ☐ A – Lawn bowls
   - ☐ B – Motor racing
   - ☐ C – Snooker
   - ☐ D – Target shooting

3. A cricket player begins training more frequently. Which training principle are they using? [1]
   - ☐ A – Individual needs
   - ☐ B – Progressive overload
   - ☐ C – Reversibility
   - ☐ D – Specificity

4. Which pair of fitness tests assess cardiovascular fitness? [1]
   - ☐ A – 30m sprint test and the press-up test
   - ☐ B – Cooper 12-minute run/swim test and the 30m sprint test
   - ☐ C – Cooper 12-minute run/swim test and the Harvard step test
   - ☐ D – Sit and reach test and the Harvard step test

5. Jack is 16. Which **one** of the following is Jack's maximum heart rate? [1]
   - ☐ A – 184
   - ☐ B – 204
   - ☐ C – 206
   - ☐ D – 236

6. (a) Which **one** of the following performance-enhancing drugs increases muscle mass? [1]
   - ☐ A – Anabolic steroids
   - ☐ B – Beta blockers
   - ☐ C – Diuretics
   - ☐ D – Stimulants

   (b) Give **two** advantages to a boxer of taking stimulants. [2]

7. Some sports performers require power.
   (a) What is meant by 'power'? [1]
   (b) Suggest **one** sporting activity where power would be an advantage. [1]
   (c) Give **one** suitable test for power. [1]

8. Agility, balance, fast reaction time, strength and coordination are all useful components of fitness for a tennis player.
   (a) Name **one** other component of fitness useful to a tennis player.
       Outline why this is important for a tennis player. [2]
   (b) Define coordination. Discuss the importance of coordination for a tennis player. [3]

9. David and Elizabeth have been taking the Illinois agility run test as part of their hockey club training. They are both 16 years old. David's time was 17.1 seconds. Elizabeth's time was 17.2 seconds.
   Analyse the data in Table 1. What does it show about David and Elizabeth's performance and level of agility? [3]

Performance category	Males aged 16–19 (sec)	Females aged 16–19 (sec)
Excellent	< 15.2	< 17.0
Good	15.2–16.1	17.0–17.9
Average	16.2–18.1	18.0–21.7
Fair	18.2–18.3	21.8–23.0
Poor	> 18.3	> 23.0

Table 1: National standards for the Illinois agility test

10. An outdoor activity centre offers rock climbing and kayaking. They have competitive teams for both sports that compete against people from other centres.
    The centre trainer has decided to use a handgrip dynamometer test to measure the strength of competitors in both sports.
    (a) Describe how to carry out this test. [3]
    (b) Evaluate whether the test is more relevant to a rock climber or a kayaker. [6]

11. Callum is a football player representing his local team. He warms up well using stretching techniques and has read that plyometric training could be used to improve his performance.
    (a) Give **three** factors other than stretching and warm-ups that Callum can use to help prevent injury in match play and training. [3]
    (b) Discuss the appropriateness of plyometric training for Callum and any other factors he might consider to improve his performance. [6]

12. Warming up mentally prepares an athlete for a period of intense fitness and skills training.
    Explain the physical effect on the body of warming up before training or exercise. [2]

13. Sam is responsible for safety at a training centre.
    Complete the table below by identifying an example and potential injuries. [3]

Factor in injury prevention	Examples	Potential injuries
Application of the principles of training.	Progressive overload not applied correctly.	(i)
Personal protective equipment.	(ii)	(iii)

14. Give **one** reason why a personal trainer would ask a client to complete a PARQ assessment before activity commences. [1]

TOPICS FOR PAPER 2
Health and Performance (1PE0/02)

Information about Component 2

Mandatory written exam: 1 hour 15 minutes
60 marks
24% of the qualification grade
Externally assessed.

All questions are mandatory.
Use black ink. You can use an HB pencil, but only for graphs and diagrams.
Calculators are permitted in this examination.

Specification coverage

Topic 1: Health, fitness and well-being

Topic 2: Sport psychology

Topic 3: Socio-cultural influences

Topic 4: Use of data

Questions

The assessment consists of multiple-choice, short-answer, long-answer and one extended writing question.

The use of data is embedded throughout the paper where appropriate.

PHYSICAL HEALTH

Physical health and wellbeing is defined as having all body systems working well, and being free from illness and injury with the ability to carry out everyday tasks.

For more on the definitions of health and fitness, see **page 35**.

Health benefits of physical fitness training

Increasing physical ability, through improving the components of fitness (see **pages 36–37**) can improve health and reduce health risks in the following ways:

Cardiovascular fitness

- Increased cardiovascular fitness will improve heart function and lower the resting heart rate.
- Blood pressure and cholesterol levels are reduced.
- The efficiency of the body's systems is improved through physical activity.

Resistance to disease

- A stronger heart reduces the risk of coronary heart disease (CHD) or stroke.
- Improved body composition and maintenance of the correct body weight helps to avoid obesity and reduces the risk of illness, e.g. type 2 diabetes or cancer.
- Resistance training can increase bone density, reducing chances of osteoporosis later in life.

Strength and endurance

- Greater muscular strength and cardiovascular endurance means people are able to do everyday tasks without tiring.
- Posture is improved.

Physical, emotional and social health are all linked, working in conjunction with each other.

1.1.2 **1.1.3** **1.1.4**

EMOTIONAL AND SOCIAL HEALTH

Emotional health and wellbeing is defined as how we think and feel about ourselves and others. This includes the ability to cope with life events, our own emotions and those of others in order to realise our own potential.

Emotional health benefits of fitness training

Exercise can make you feel good. Participation in physical activity and sport can improve emotional and psychological health.

- Exercise releases endorphins and serotonin, neurotransmitters in the body that make you feel good. This reduces stress, tension and anxiety.
- Exercise can provide a sense of achievement and fulfilment which can increase confidence and self-esteem.
- Exercise helps to alleviate depression.
- Exercise helps people to control their emotions or anger.

Sport can also be appreciated for its aesthetic qualities and elegance of movement.

Some movements can be beautiful, for example a well-executed freestyle skiing trick, a slam dunk in basketball or an amazing tennis shot.

Social health benefits of fitness training

Social health and wellbeing means that basic human needs are being met (for example, food, shelter and clothing). The individual has friendship and support, some value in society, is socially active and has little stress in social circumstances.

Physical activity and sport often:
- Provides opportunities to socialise and make friends.
- Involves playing in a team which requires cooperation and teamwork. It also encourages communication between team members and a feeling of achieving a common goal.

---

1. Participating in physical activity and sport can improve health.
   Complete the table below, stating the type of health benefit for each row. [3]

Benefit	Type of health benefit
Making friends	(a) Social (health)[1]
Improved cardiovascular endurance	(b) Physical (health)[1]
Increased confidence	(c) Emotional (health)[1]

2. Explain **two** negative benefits of fitness on well-being. [4]

Over-training or overuse of the body may make you more prone to injury.[1] Being unable to train / having time off as a result of an injury can cause depression and longer-term health problems.[1]

Competitive sport can add undue pressure to perform[1] which can result in psychological issues and a loss of confidence / stress related illness.[1]

Physical activity can alter body composition in ways which are not healthy[1] or lead to an unhealthy emotional obsession with shape, e.g. anorexia.[1]

HOW TO PROMOTE PERSONAL HEALTH

Personal health can be promoted through the use of a **personal exercise programme** (**PEP**). This should be carefully designed, developed, monitored and evaluated to meet the specific needs of an individual.

Personal Exercise Programme (PEP)

1 Design

A PEP needs to be carefully designed to suit the specific needs and goals of an individual.

Based on information from a PARQ assessment (**page 54**) and a baseline fitness test, it should provide the right amount of challenge without overstretching an individual, with exercises that are carefully matched to the desired outcomes and components of fitness.

2 Development

Over time, the PEP can be developed to extend the level of challenge or to include different exercises to cater for more developed goals.

3 Monitoring

Participation in the exercises developed in the plan should be monitored and recorded to be able to evaluate the effectiveness of the programme and to make necessary adjustments and ongoing perfections.

4 Evaluation

In the evaluation stage, the post PEP data can be compared with the baseline data to see where improvements have been made. This helps to identify where changes should be made and why.

Changes help to ensure progression, to encourage motivation and to provide sufficient challenge.

Explain how a personal exercise programme can promote health for an individual. [2]

A PEP provides reassurance[1] that a programme is going to have positive outcomes for an individual / that the time and physical exertion will be worth it,[1] and that the exercises are suitable for the individual's level of fitness.[1] A PEP can encourage an individual to train more often[1] and to take more of an interest / care in their fitness levels.[1]

1.1.6 1.1.7

LIFESTYLE CHOICES IN DIET, ACTIVITY LEVEL AND THE WORK / REST / SLEEP BALANCE

Our lifestyle choices can greatly impact our own lifespan and general health.

Diet and activity

A balanced diet is defined as eating the right type and the right amount of nutrients that your body requires, consuming only as many calories as your body burns each day at rest (your **basal metabolic rate**) and through activity. Excess calories are stored as fat. A calorie deficit can cause a reduction of body mass through fat and muscle loss.

Increasing the amount of exercise you do will require an increase in calories and nutrients, for example, additional protein to help muscle growth.

A lifestyle choice to increase your activity can improve your physical, emotional and social health. See page 69.

Work / rest / sleep balance

In order to work and exercise effectively, a minimum of eight hours sleep per night is recommended to allow the brain and body systems to recover and replenish after the day's activities.

The negative impacts of a chronic (long-term) lack of **sleep** include **raised blood pressure** and an increased risk of **heart disease**, **stroke**, **diabetes**, **kidney disease** and **obesity**.

Give **two** consequences of a poor diet on participation in physical activity and sport. [2]

Two from: tiredness,[1] growth related issues / reduced strength,[1] reduced motivation,[1] reduced speed through obesity / lethargy,[1] slower response / reaction times.[1] Accept other valid responses.

Edexcel GCSE **Physical Education** — Paper 2, Topic 1

1.1.6 1.1.7

LIFESTYLE CHOICES IN RELATION TO LEGAL RECREATIONAL DRUGS

Legal recreational drugs include nicotine and alcohol. Each affect the body and its ability to perform in different ways. Long term use or abuse can have severe consequences.

Alcohol

Alcohol is a **depressant** that causes your body's responses to slow down. Long term or heavy consumption of alcohol can result in **liver damage**.

The side effects of drinking alcohol before participation in sport include:
- Dehydration which can result in dizziness and headaches, reducing alertness and concentration.
- Reduced reaction times which can result in injury or poorer performance.
- Reduced blood glucose levels which reduces the performance of muscles and increases the onset of fatigue.

Figure 1 shows the average percentage of males and females in England who drink more than the recommended maximum units of alcohol per week.

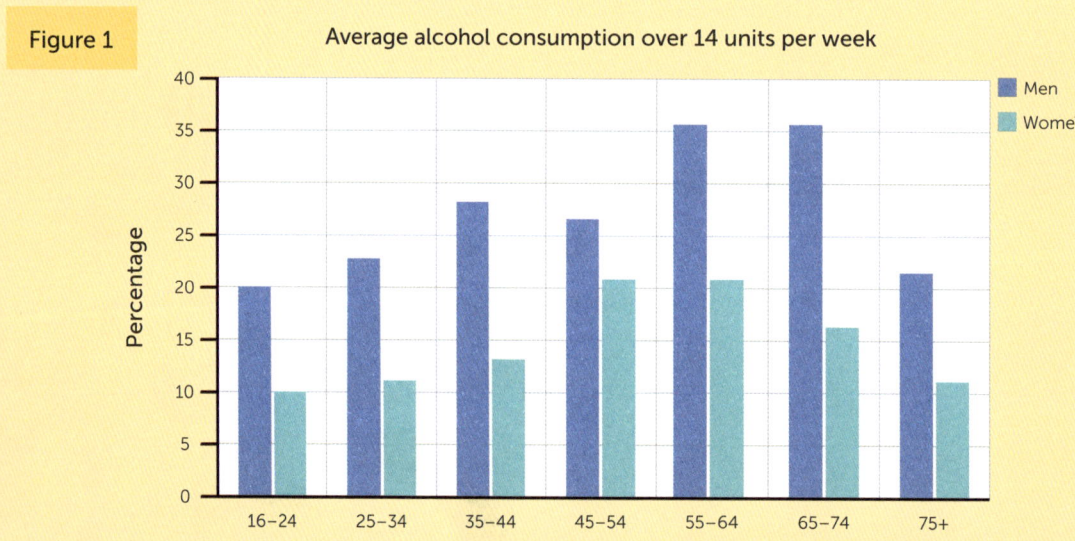

Figure 1

(a) Identify the percentage of 45–54 year old women who consume more than 14 units of alcohol per week. [1]
(b) Identify the age group of men with the lowest percentage of alcohol consumption. [1]

(a) 21% (Allow ±1 variation).
(b) 16–24 year olds.

Smoking

Nicotine in cigarettes is a **stimulant** that increases alertness, however, it is **highly addictive** and comes with a long list of serious side effects including **bronchitis** and **lung cancer**. Choosing to smoke will also impact performance in physical activity and sports in the following ways:

- Reduces the oxygen carrying capacity of red blood cells.
- Gaseous exchange becomes less effective, reducing oxygen into the bloodstream for energy production.
- Diffusion of oxygen in the lungs and muscles decreases, affecting aerobic capacity and increasing fatigue.
- Reduces lung capacity.

See **pages 16 and 20** for more on gaseous exchange and diffusion.

1.2

THE CONSEQUENCES OF A SEDENTARY LIFESTYLE

Our **lifestyle** is the way in which we choose to live. This includes choices over what to consume, how often to exercise and decisions over employment. A **sedentary lifestyle** is one with little, irregular or no physical activity.

Consequences of a sedentary lifestyle

A sedentary lifestyle can involve spending long periods in front of the TV or sitting at a desk. This increases the risk of long-term health complications. Possible consequences of a sedentary lifestyle include:

Physical health

- Weight gain or obesity
- Coronary heart disease (CHD)
- Hypertension (high blood pressure)
- Diabetes
- Increased risk of osteoporosis
- Poor sleep
- Poor posture owing to a loss of muscle tone
- Impacts on the components of fitness.

Emotional health

- Poor self-esteem
- Depression
- Lethargy.

Social health

- Fewer opportunities to socialise.

Society and modern conveniences have contributed to a more sedentary lifestyle.

For example, having greater access to cars and buses instead of walking or cycling, using labour saving devices such as dishwashers and robotic lawnmowers, or having a preference for video games and television over the great outdoors.

1. Explain **two** ways in which a sedentary lifestyle can impact physical health and wellbeing. [4]

A lack of exercise can result in consuming more calories than are burned through exercise,[1] leading to weight gain.[1] If the heart does not get exercise, it gets weaker and has to work harder / fatty deposits can build up in the arteries,[1] leading to hypertension / heart disease.[1] A lack of exercise can cause muscle cells to lose their sensitivity to insulin,[1] causing diabetes.[1] Exercise helps to prevent insomnia / reduces stress / resets the body clock[1] to improve sleep.[1] Reduced weight bearing exercise can lead to a loss of muscle tone,[1] causing poor posture / limited mobility / brittle bones (osteoporosis),[1] increasing the chances of injury / fractures and breaks.[1]

Obesity and performance

Obesity is defined as having a body mass index (BMI) of over 30 or over 20% above standard weight for height ratio. Obese people have a large fat content, caused by an imbalance of calories consumed to energy expenditure.

Being **overweight** means carrying excess body fat but not to the extent of being obese. The term '**overfat**' refers to the presences of excess body fat that can impair health, even in individuals who are not overweight.

Obesity:

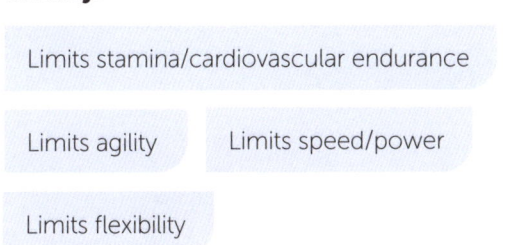

BMI (Body Mass Index) is not on the specification, but it provides a rough approximation of obesity.

Use the chart below to calculate your BMI.

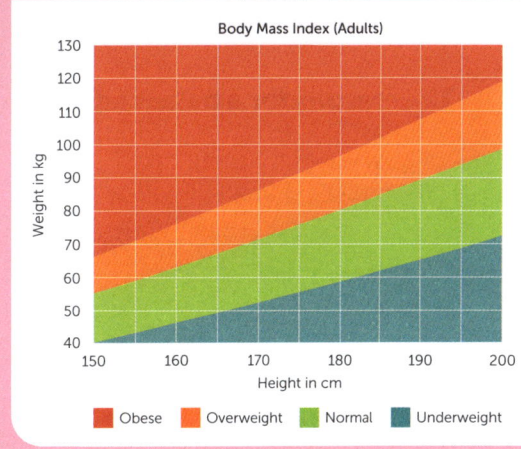

---

2. Explain **two** ways that obesity could negatively impact performance in football or rugby. [2]
3. Using the BMI chart, assess the BMI rating for an adult of 80kg who is 180cm in height. Make recommendations for their lifestyle choices. [2]
4. Using **Figure 1**, identify the year in which adult blood pressure was at its highest since 2010. [1]

Figure 1

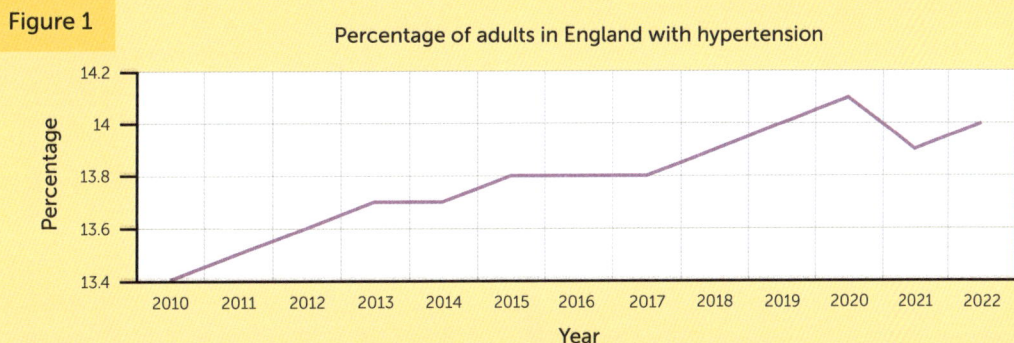

2. Limits stamina/cardiovascular endurance so a player cannot complete an entire game.[1] Limits flexibility so reduces the ability to reach/control a ball.[1] Limits agility so a player is less able to change direction/sidestep to avoid an opponent.[1] Limits speed/power so a player is less able to keep up with the ball / more likely to get tackled / cannot leap high enough to head the ball or in a line-out.[1]

3. Normal weight.[1] Since their BMI is close to being overweight, they may consider increasing their levels of exercise / decreasing their calorific intake.[1]

4. 2020.[1]

Edexcel GCSE **Physical Education** — Paper 2, Topic 1

1.3.1

BALANCED DIET

A **balanced diet** contains lots of different types of food to provide the right nutrients, vitamins and minerals required by your body.

Nutrition is defined as the intake of food, considered in relation to the body's dietary needs. Good nutrition is an adequate, well-balanced diet, combined with regular physical activity.

The reasons for a balanced diet

1. The body needs sufficient calorific energy available for its activity.
2. The body needs the correct nutrients for growth and hydration.
3. Consuming too much can create unused, or surplus, energy which is stored as fat. This could cause obesity (particularly with saturated fat).
4. To make sure that we get the right vitamins and minerals to prevent diseases such as rickets or scurvy.

The ratio of carbohydrates, fat and protein

A balanced diet contains roughly 55–60% carbohydrate, 25–30% fat, 15–20% protein.

This can come from eating a variety of fruits and vegetables; bread, rice and pasta; meat, fish and eggs; and milk and dairy products.

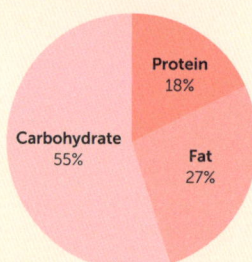

Protein 18%
Carbohydrate 55%
Fat 27%

1. Which **one** of the following meals provides the best balance of nutrients for a distance cyclist the day before a major competition? [1]
   A – Four cheese macaroni with sausage
   B – Bacon, lettuce and tomato sandwich
   C – Grilled chicken, leek and sweet potato pasta with broccoli
   D – Vegetable stir fry with rice

   C.[1] (Balance of carbohydrates for energy, protein for muscle repair, rich in vitamins and minerals and low in fat.)

2. Explain why a sprinter may need a diet of high carbohydrates and protein. [4]

   Carbohydrates are burned at varying intensities, unlike fat, so their body can break down the carbohydrates into glucose for increased energy during intense training and competition.[1] Carbohydrates would therefore be the preferred energy source of the body.[1] Protein helps to develop muscular strength so they can increase their power and race times.[1] Outside of training and competition, the muscles require protein to repair themselves.[1]

THE ROLE AND IMPORTANCE OF MACRONUTRIENTS

Macronutrients are the major food types that are consumed to maintain a healthy balanced diet.

Macronutrients

Carbohydrates

Carbohydrates are the main and preferred **energy** source for all types of exercise. They also provide energy when working at any level of intensity.

Protein

Protein is for the **growth and repair** of muscle tissue, developing muscular strength.

Fat

Fats are essential for the body, though some types are better than others. Fat provides more **energy** than carbohydrates but only at **low intensity**, for example walking or jogging.

Fat provides **insulation** for the body, it protects vital organs with additional **cushioning** and supports **cell growth**.

Carbohydrate loading

Carbohydrate loading is a strategy used by distance or endurance athletes to increase energy stores before a major event. They commonly reduce their training levels and consume large amounts of carbohydrates before a race to preserve the existing glycogen stores in their muscles and boost additional reserves. This means that they can maintain their pace for longer, improving their overall performance.

Timing of protein intake

Power athletes, such as weightlifters, time their **protein intake** soon after exercise to allow their muscles to **repair and grow** (**hypertrophy**) more quickly by **increasing protein synthesis**. (Proteins consumed are broken down and transformed into new proteins to form new muscle fibres.) Athletes commonly consume protein shakes or bars as an immediate snack after training.

THE ROLE AND IMPORTANCE OF MICRONUTRIENTS

Micronutrients should be consumed in small amounts and are essential for growth and general health.

Micronutrients

Vitamins

Vitamins, for example A, B1, C, D and E, help to **prevent disease** and assist in the production of energy. They are essential for **metabolism** and aid tissue growth and repair.

Water

Water is necessary for good **hydration**. It replaces fluids lost during exercise and improves physical and mental performance.

Fibre

Fibre **aids digestion**, **reduces cholesterol**, and limits obesity, diabetes and certain cancers.

Minerals

Minerals are vital to maintain the efficient working of the body's systems and for general health.

- **Calcium** is important for bone growth.
- **Iron** is known to improve the oxygen carrying capacity of blood cells.
- **Zinc** promotes healing and cell growth. It also strengthens the immune system to help fight off illness.
- **Potassium** and **sulfur** are also essential micronutrients.

Rickets is caused by a lack of vitamin D and calcium affecting bone development or weakening them in adults.

Scurvy is caused by a lack of vitamin C, causing tiredness, joint pain and bleeding gums.

Explain, with the use of an example, how a sprinter benefits from getting the correct vitamins in their diet. [3]

Vitamins helps to maintain basic body functions.[1] Vitamin C helps to fight infection[1] so that the athlete does not suffer time away from training through illness.[1] Vitamin D helps regulate the absorption of calcium[1] to help maintain stronger bones which helps avoid injury, fracture or break.[1]

THE FACTORS AFFECTING OPTIMUM WEIGHT

The factors that affect an athlete's optimum weight include **gender**, **height**, **bone structure** and **muscle** (girth).

Variation in optimum weight

Depending on an athlete's chosen sport, playing position or specialism, they may change their optimum weight to best suit the requirements of the specific physical activity.

Equally, a person with a naturally smaller bone structure and shorter height may find they have an advantage in one sport over another, for example, a jockey. A high jump athlete will typically have a very different optimum weight to a shot putter. They will also likely vary in height, bone structure and muscle mass.

Energy balance

Energy balance describes the amount of energy consumed compared to the amount of energy used (burned off) by the body. To maintain a healthy weight, the *energy in* (in food) should equal the *energy out*, otherwise the body will gain or lose weight. See **page 71** for more details.

Men typically have a greater bone structure and muscle mass than women of the same height.

Explain how the optimum weight of a marathon runner would differ from that of a 100m sprinter. [3]

A marathon runner would ideally be lighter in weight compared to a sprinter[1] to avoid carrying additional mass[1] over a long distance. Sprinters tend to be taller than distance runners[1] so that they get greater leverage and power from longer legs,[1] whereas marathon runners benefit from shorter legs which don't weigh as much.[1] Sprinter have more developed muscle mass[1] to provide the burst of explosive power they need over the short distance.[1] Distance runners have a lighter bone structure which reduces weight.[1]

Edexcel GCSE **Physical Education — Paper 2, Topic 1**

HYDRATION FOR PHYSICAL ACTIVITY AND SPORT

People need to have enough water for their bodies to function normally. **Dehydration** refers to an excessive loss of body water, interrupting the function of the body. Rehydrating means to consume water to restore correct levels. Hydration can involve pre-hydration prior to a sporting event.

Consequences of dehydration

Blood will thicken (increase in **viscosity**) with less water content, which slows blood flow, meaning less oxygen is supplied to the working muscles and to the brain, potentially causing headaches.

It also means that waste products such as CO_2 and lactic acid cannot be removed as efficiently.

The heart will have to work harder, as a result of blood thickening, to supply oxygen to the working muscles during exercise. It may also develop an irregular rhythm. This could result in a poorer performance for a sports person.

Reaction times slow down as the brain is receiving less oxygen and muscles get tired. This can result in poor decision making and reduced skill levels.

The body could increase in temperature (overheat) as a result of a lack of water available for sweating, causing dizziness or fainting. This could prevent a performer from continuing their training or activity.

Muscles will tire, causing fatigue, cramps, a limited range of movement and potentially preventing activity from continuing.

A sprinter from the Bahamas pulled up with cramp in the Women's 200m semi-final of the IAAF World Championships at The Khalifa International Stadium, Doha, Qatar.

(a) Give **one** cause of cramp. [1]

(b) Explain how the sprinter may have adjusted her water intake for the championships in the hot, dry climate in Qatar. [1]

(a) *Dehydration / tired muscles / insufficient oxygen to the working muscles.*[1]

(b) *Increase water intake*[1] *in order to compensate for increased loss of water through sweating / increased evaporation in the breath.*[1] *Pre-hydration.*[1]

EXAMINATION PRACTICE

1. Which **one** of the following is a benefit of emotional health and wellbeing? [1]
   - ☐ A – Improved heart function
   - ☐ B – More able to complete everyday tasks
   - ☐ C – Reduced risk of illness
   - ☐ D – Reduced stress

For questions 2 and 3, use the information in Figure 1 to decide if A, B , C or D is correct.

Figure 1 shows the percentage of smokers in the UK between 2011 and 2021.

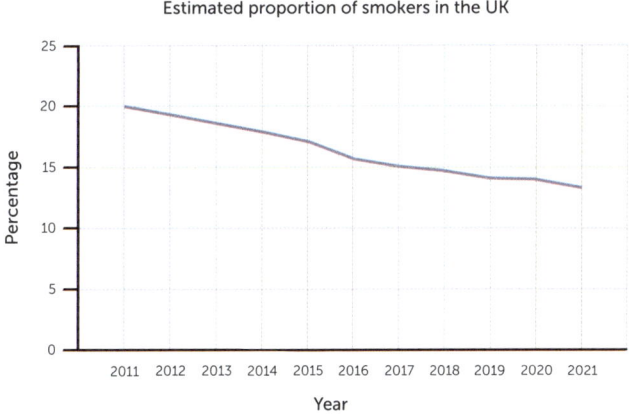

Figure 1

2. Which **one** of the following shows the trend in smoking over the decade? [1]
   - ☐ A – Constant
   - ☐ B – Gradual decline
   - ☐ C – Gradual increase
   - ☐ D – Sharp increase

3. Identify the year in which the proportion of smokers first dropped below 15%. [1]
   - ☐ A – 2011
   - ☐ B – 2016
   - ☐ C – 2018
   - ☐ D – 2021

4. Participating in sports improves social health and wellbeing.
   - (a) Define social health and wellbeing. [1]
   - (b) State **two** positive effects that being physically active can have on social health and wellbeing. [2]
   - (c) Explain how better health could help improve fitness. [2]

5. Simon is designing a personal exercise programme for a student he coaches.
   Explain **one** consideration he should make in the design of the programme. [2]

6. A balanced diet requires that fats, proteins and carbohydrates are consumed in the right proportions.
   (a) State the percentage of fats that should be consumed in a balanced diet. [1]
   (b) Give **one** health risk as a result of consuming more than the recommended fat percentage. [1]
   (c) State **one** way in which a person's fat content can be reduced. [1]
   (d) An adult has decided to reduce their BMI. Table 2 shows their progress over 6 months. Plot the BMI points onto the graph below and draw a line between them showing the trend. Label the axes. [2]

	Jan	Feb	Mar	Apr	May	Jun
BMI score	28	26	25	24	23.5	23

Table 1

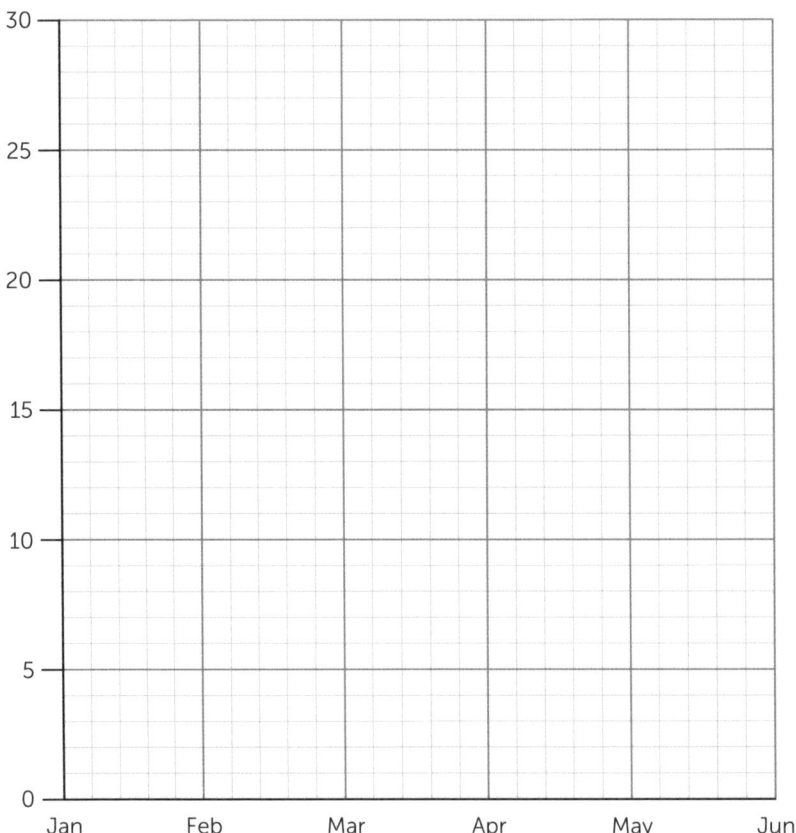

7. During his 21-day Tour de France race, Chris Froome reportedly consumed 8000 calories per day.

(a) Explain **one** reason why performers may need to increase their calorific intake. [2]

(b) Describe how Chris may have maintained hydration during the race. [2]

(c) Explain how dehydration may impact the heart and blood flow of a performer. [2]

2.1
CLASSIFICATION OF SKILLS

Different sports require different sets of skills for performers to acquire and perfect.

Skill and ability

A **skill** is a learned action or learned behaviour with the intention of bringing about predetermined results, with maximum certainty and minimum outlay of time and energy.

An **ability** is an inherited, stable trait that determines an individual's potential to learn or acquire a skill.

Classifications of skill

Skills can be classified in three ways:

Difficulty continuum: Basic to complex

A **basic** (**simple**) **skill** (e.g. *jogging*) requires few decisions to be made that affect the skill so they are learned quickly and require a low level of coordination or concentration to complete.

A **complex skill** (e.g. *batting in cricket*) requires lots of decisions in order to be successful and requires a high level of coordination and concentration.

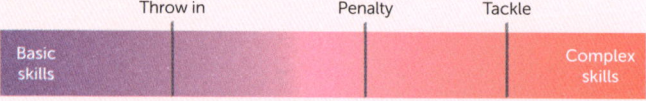

Environmental continuum: Open to closed

An **open skill** (e.g. *football tackle*) is performed in a certain way to deal with a changing or unstable environment, e.g. the position or movement of an opponent will affect how you should tackle them.

A **closed skill** (e.g. *platform dive*) is one which is not affected by the environment or performers within it. The skill tends to be done the same way each time.

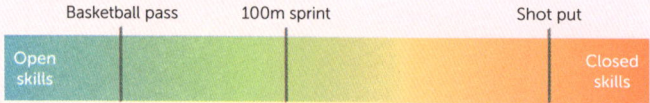

Organisational continuum: Low to high

A **low organisational skill** (e.g. *swimming*) can be separated into its constituent parts so that each can be practiced individually, for example, the dive, the glide, the stroke, and the turn.

A **high organisational skill** (e.g. *a golf drive*) has a complex set of skills that cannot be separated so they must be practised together.

Massed and distributed practice

Massed practice

Massed practice involves little or no breaks. The sessions tend to be long and intensive and practice continues until the skill has been learned. Massed practice works best with fit and experienced athletes.

- ➕ Best for elite performers
- ➕ Can quickly create the feeling or pattern of a movement
- ➕ Provides time to focus on a particular skill
- ➕ Useful for skills that are basic, closed and of low organisation.
- ➖ Can get repetitive, tiring and boring
- ➖ Performance may drop owing to fatigue
- ➖ Requires a lot of motivation
- ➖ No time for feedback

Distributed practice

Distributed practice allows the performer to take breaks during the practice. Breaks allow for rest, to receive feedback and provide time for reflection.

- ➕ Best for performers who are less physically fit as breaks aid recovery
- ➕ More varied and provides opportunity to adapt ability to different situations
- ➕ Suitable for beginners who need time for feedback between training sessions
- ➕ Useful for skills that are complex, open and of high organisation.
- ➖ Takes longer to embed a skill given the stop/start nature
- ➖ Will not build muscle memory
- ➖ Does not replicate the physical demand for elite performers
- ➖ Performers may lose focus or momentum owing to breaks

Fixed and variable practice

Fixed practice repeats a skill over and over again as a whole movement so that it becomes engrained. The skill is often **closed** and of **high organisational** level so cannot be, or is not, broken down into smaller steps.

Variable practice suits **open**, **low organisational** skills where the skills can be practiced in a variety of different situations. This can help a performer to adapt their skills to the environment and to increase the level of difficulty.

Skills can be classified on a continuum. A skill may lie somewhere on a line between one extreme and the other.

You may need to justify why a skill is nearer one end than another.

A golf shot is placed on a difficulty continuum below. Justify, using examples, why the golf shot has not been placed nearer to the closed end of the scale. [4]

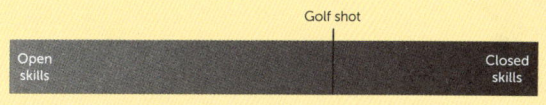

Closed skills are unaffected by the environment.[1] In golf, conditions are not always identical.[1] Wind speed and direction can influence the address and set up of the shot.[1] Rain can make the club handle slippery which may affect the grip strength.[1] Crowd noise can affect concentration levels.[1] The height and lay of the ball will affect the stance.[1]

2.2

GOAL SETTING WITH SMART TARGETS

Sporting goals vary according to what the performer wants to achieve. Goals can be set by athletes themselves, or by their coaches.

SMART targets

SMART targets are appropriately defined goals that can be used to improve and/or **optimise performance**. They can **motivate performers** to achieve **exercise goals**, provide additional **interest** in activity, and help **adherence to training**. Goals can also **reduce stress** and **improve focus**.

S — Specific
Goals must be specific to the demands of the sport, the muscles or the movements used.

M — Measurable
It must be possible to measure whether a goal has been met.

A — Achievable
Goals should actually be possible to complete / within capability.

R — Realistic
Goals can be achieved given the available time and resources.

T — Time-bound
A set period of time or deadline by which the goal will be achieved.

Beginner skier

Goal: To link 15 turns using parallel skis by the end of one week.

- **S** — Specific to the stage that the skier is at in their learning.
- **M** — I will ski for four hours each day to achieve 15 linked turns.
- **A** — The skier feels that they have the capability to achieve this.
- **R** — This is what people are expected to do in one week of lessons.
- **T** — To be achieved by the end of the week.

Downhill racer

Goal: To reduce my first split time by 0.6 seconds within 28 days.

- **S** — Improve my start time by keeping my poles nearer my feet for a faster split in the top section.
- **M** — To shave off an average 0.6s from the first split time.
- **A** — The coach feels the skier can achieve this and is getting better.
- **R** — A good start can improve a race time by up to 2s so this is possible.
- **T** — To achieve it in 28 days of practice.

---

1. Nina says she wants to improve her golf handicap.
   (a) Identify **one** way in which she can make this goal SMART. [1]
   (b) Explain why Nina should review her targets after a set period of time. [2]

(a) Specific – Nina needs to state how many points she wants to reduce the handicap by / the target handicap.[1] Achievable – Nina needs to be confident that she is capable of reaching her goal in the time given.[1] Realistic – The goal should be achievable given the available time and resources (e.g. coaching).[1] Time bound – Nina needs to state a date by when the goal should be met.[1] The goal is already measurable.

(b) To compare actual results with the original targets[1] which will provide feedback on progress[1] / in order to make adaptations to training as required[1] / to boost motivation.[1]

TYPES OF GUIDANCE

Coaches need to identify the most appropriate methods to provide guidance to beginners or elite level performers to aid the learning of a skill.

Types of guidance

Visual (seeing)

Visual guidance involves the use of demonstrations that allow the performer to 'see' the skill. This includes watching an instructor, video, images or diagrams.

- ⊕ Quick and concise which is good for beginners to create a mental picture that they can copy
- ⊕ Slow motion replays can be used for detailed analysis of complex skills
- ⊖ Complex skills can be difficult to demonstrate clearly
- ⊖ Performers need to be paying close attention.

Verbal (hearing)

Coaches or instructors will provide explanations of how to do things, or audible cues on when to move or hold a position.

- ⊕ Can be provided whilst a sporting action is being performed
- ⊕ Easily combined with other forms of guidance
- ⊖ Less suitable for beginners if technical language is used
- ⊖ Complex skills are difficult to explain in words.

Types of guidance continued

Manual (Physical assistance with movement)

Coaches may physically manipulate the athlete through the skill by moving body parts into the correct position, stance or through a complete range of motion.

- ⊕ Useful for beginners to get the feel of a movement or position, or for safety
- ⊕ Subtle positioning can be adjusted to develop complex skills
- ⊖ Useful on an individual basis only rather than with sports teams
- ⊖ Less suitable for elite performers
- ⊖ Physical contact requires consent.

Mechanical (use of objects or aids)

Sports equipment is used to assist the performer, for example, swimming paddles, arm bands or tennis ball machines.

- ⊕ Useful for beginners to 'feel' the motion, technique or for safety
- ⊕ Builds confidence without the fear of injury
- ⊖ Performers may come to rely on the support
- ⊖ Mistakes in technique using the aids can become engrained.

State the type of guidance being provided in each example below:
(a) A child is using stabilisers to learn to ride a bike. [1]
(b) A boxer's arms are physically moved into the correct guard positions by their coach. [1]

(a) *Mechanical.*[1]
(b) *Manual.*[1]

TYPES OF FEEDBACK TO OPTIMISE PERFORMANCE

Feedback can be given to a sportsperson either during or after their activity with the aim of improving future performances.

Types of feedback

Intrinsic (or **kinaesthetic**) **feedback** comes from within. It is 'felt' by the performer through their own senses or muscles.

Beginners do not usually have enough experience to have developed a feeling for correct technique. They cannot interpret the intrinsic feedback. Elite athletes have a strongly developed sense of their own performances that they can 'feel' and can interpret the feedback.

Extrinsic feedback is provided by someone else, commonly a coach, parent, spectator or team captain.

This is useful for beginners who are less aware of what a successful technique looks or feels like, and when they don't know how to improve. Elite performers may combine extrinsic and intrinsic feedback

Concurrent feedback is provided during a performance and can be acted on immediately e.g. *"Good positioning, pass to David"*.

Terminal feedback is provided at the end of a performance, e.g. *"Keep your chin tucked in next time"*.

1. **Figure 1** shows the placement and percentages of successful first serves and aces for an elite tennis player during a set.
   Analyse the data and suggest **one** strength and **one** weakness of the player. [2]

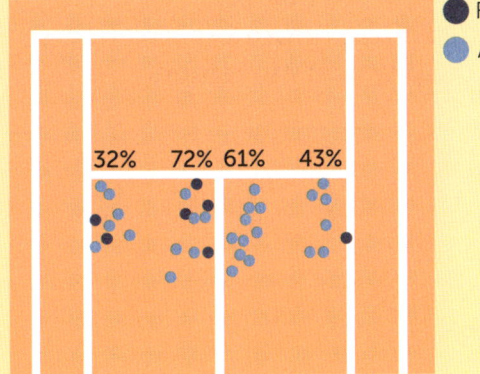

Figure 1

2. Dana is a competitive weight lifter. She uses a wall mirror when she is training in the gym.
   Explain why an athlete might use a mirror as a training tool. [2]

3. Evaluate the importance of concurrent and terminal feedback for members of an under 13s youth cricket team. [9]

---

1. Better at serving aces to the left of the court.[1] Stronger at serving to the centre of the court.[1] Lowest number of successful shots across to the left of the court.[1] No aces scored in the centre right of the court.[1]

2. A mirror provides an instant knowledge of performance[1] which helps to develop / fine tune technique.[1] Extrinsic feedback from the mirror[1] can help to develop / fine tune intrinsic feedback.[1]

3. **Knowledge and understanding of concurrent and terminal feedback (AO1)**
   Concurrent feedback is provided whilst the skills is being performed[✓] so that it can be acted on immediately.[✓] Terminal feedback is provided at the end of the performance[✓], commonly as a summary[✓] so that performance can be improved next time in light of the feedback.[✓]

   Application of knowledge and understanding (AO2)
   An example of concurrent feedback is a parent or coach shouting at batters to "slide the bat into the crease" during a run.[✓] It can also reinforce correct action e.g. "great catch".[✓] An example of terminal feedback is being given the match statistics for a bowler compared to their prior performances / being told to work on increasing their pace for the next match.[✓] Concurrent feedback is used for immediate effect on skills that are slow enough for the performer to respond to the feedback during the action.[✓] Terminal feedback is used to provide a broader summary of the game / for reflection.[✓]

   Evaluation of the merits of concurrent and terminal feedback (AO3)
   Concurrent feedback is useful for younger, more inexperienced players as they can make corrections and get further feedback as they go.[✓] They can also feel the immediate effect of any positive changes.[✓] Feedback can reinforce corrective action which may improve performance.[✓] Praise / affirmation of a correct movement provides valuable motivation for the players / team.[✓] Too much concurrent feedback may overload players which could decrease levels of performance.[✓] Terminal feedback can provide a summary of results compared to an earlier match strategy which can help future matches.[✓]

   This question should be marked in accordance with the levels based mark scheme on page 123.

MENTAL PREPARATION FOR PERFORMANCE

Mental preparation is used by performers to rehearse a physical skill in their head without any actual physical movement.

Warm up

Warm ups provide an opportunity for performers' muscles to 'remember' the correct actions, for them to 'get into the swing' of their activities and to put them into the right mental (and physical) zone in preparation for sports or physical activity.

In team sports, a warm up together can reignite the sense of unity and communication required for a successful performance. The correct mindset before competition can greatly improve outcomes in sport.

Mental rehearsal

By mentally picturing themselves performing a skill perfectly and imagining positive outcomes before attempting it (such as a podium finish), sportspeople can **reduce their stress**, improving their **confidence** and **focus** on their performance. These are common techniques used by performers such as long- and high-jumpers, football players before a penalty kick, or divers before leaving the platform. This gives them time to think through their technique, to form a successful strategy and to prepare themselves for the action.

Visualisation and **imagery** can also be used to imagine being in a calm, relaxing environment, blocking out the noise and pressure from a large audience for example.

A Belgian athlete mentally rehearsing the women's heptathlon shot put.

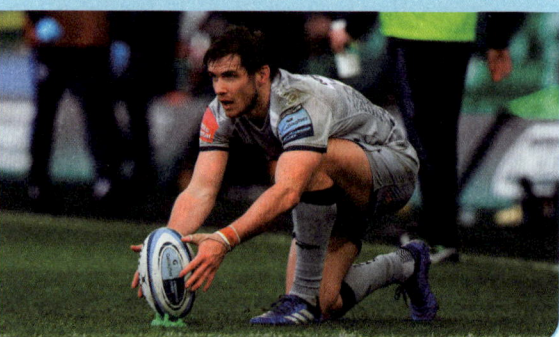

A rugby player uses visualisation and imagery before taking a conversion kick.

Give **one** advantage of mental rehearsal to an athlete in advance of competition. [1]

One from: Reduce stress / anxiety.[1] Improve confidence.[1] Increase concentration.[1] To get 'into the zone'.[1]

Paper 2, Topic 2

EXAMINATION PRACTICE

1. Which **one** of the following is an example of manual guidance? [1]
   - ☐ A – Having your hips moved over the downhill ski by an instructor
   - ☐ B – Listening to the football manager in a half time talk
   - ☐ C – Using swimming paddles to develop a cleaner and more powerful technique
   - ☐ D – Watching a coach perform a defensive shot in cricket

2. Which **one** of the following best describes massed practice? [1]
   - ☐ A – Breaking down a skill into parts to practise one element
   - ☐ B – Practising a skill repeatedly until it is learned
   - ☐ C – Practising all your skills at once
   - ☐ D – Taking regular breaks in training to allow time to recover

3. Feedback provided by a coach at the end of a training session is… [1]
   - ☐ A – Extrinsic and concurrent
   - ☐ B – Extrinsic and terminal
   - ☐ C – Intrinsic and concurrent
   - ☐ D – Intrinsic and terminal

4. Sports involve a range of skills.
   - (a) Give **one** sporting example of an open skill. Justify your answer. [3]
   - (b) Which **one** of the following tennis skills is simplest? [1]
     - ☐ A – Hitting a forehand from a stationary practice position
     - ☐ B – Making a drop shot
     - ☐ C – Returning a serve
     - ☐ D – Striking a backhand volley in match play

   Open skills ──────────────── Closed skills

   - (c) Skills can be classified as being open or closed or anywhere in between. Where on the environmental continuum would you place a long jump? Indicate by placing an X on the continuum. [1]
   - (d) Explain why closed skills tend to lend themselves more to fixed practice. [2]

5. Describe the skills involved in a cricket bowl according to **two** classifications. [2]

6. Explain **two** reasons why distributed practice would be suitable for use with a beginner golfer. [2]

7. Jo has started playing badminton with the hope of competing for her local club one day. Her instructor has provided performance goals to help her improve her accuracy and to perfect specific movements in gameplay.

   An unforced error is committed by the player in a situation where they are in full control.

   Jo has collected the following data relating to her unforced errors in recent matches:

Match	1	2	3	Target
Unforced errors	39%	34%	30%	15%

   Table 1

   (a) Explain why the instructor has set goals to help motivate Jo. [2]
   (b) Analyse the data in Table 1.
       Identify **two** ways in which Jo can make her target percentage of errors SMART. [2]
   (c) Explain **one** way in which goal setting can help to reduce injury. [2]
   (d) Jo is shown a video by her coach of a new technique to help improve her service returns.
       (i) State what type of guidance the coach is using. [1]
       (ii) Give **one** advantage and one disadvantage of this type of guidance. [2]

8. Identify and describe **one** stress management technique that could be used by a player preparing to take a conversion. [2]

9. Evaluate the effectiveness of intrinsic motivation for an elite performer in sport. [4]

ENGAGEMENT PATTERNS OF DIFFERENT SOCIAL GROUPS IN PHYSICAL ACTIVITY

Different factors affect the levels of participation and engagement of different social groups in exercise and activity based on their **personal factors**.

Social grouping by Age

Examples of factors affecting participation:

Cost

Younger people may not have the money to afford to take part in certain activities. Older people may have increased financial commitments and living costs that lower their disposable income available for activity.

Education

Time for schoolwork may come before time for evening sports clubs. Some schools offer greater sporting provision than others. People may simply not know what is available to them.

Media coverage

An increase in media coverage of older sports performers may motivate older people to take part. Most active sports people disappear from the media when they retire which is usually only in their 30s.

Discrimination

Not all clubs and memberships are available to all **ages** — some may not allow children.

---

1. The adult participation in sporting activities for different age groups is shown in **Figure 1**. Give **two** reasons why the over 75s have significantly lower levels of participation. [2]

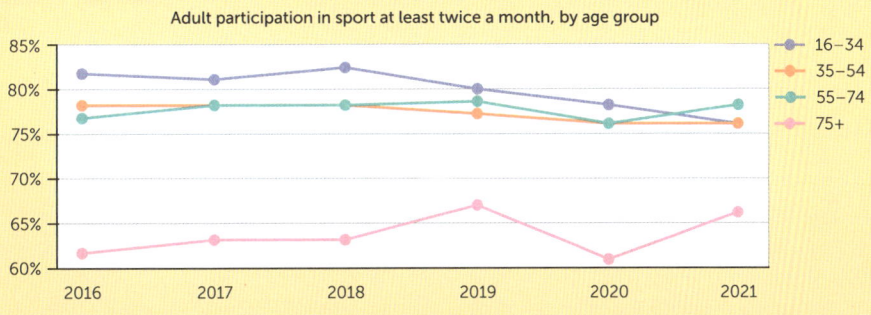

Figure 1 — Adult participation in sport at least twice a month, by age group

1. Answers may include: Illness / obesity / poor health,[1] poor mobility,[1] friends or social group do not participate,[1] lack of older role models,[1] self conscious / feel too old,[1] fear of injury,[1] lack of elderly sports groups / provision,[1] discrimination against the elderly.[1]

Social grouping by Gender

Examples of factors affecting participation:

Discrimination

Sexist or **stereotypical** attitudes may affect how comfortable (or not) woman feel about taking part. Most sports clubs now cater for both men and women, but some can still be largely male dominated, e.g. golf clubs.

Role models

There may be a lack of gender specific role models to inspire others of that gender to participate.

Accessibility

Regular sports teams for women may not always exist within a convenient travelling distance.

2019 FIFA Women's World Cup.

Media coverage

Media coverage may be more prevalent for males, compared to females.

---

2. Males are more likely to participate in sports than females. Identify **three** reasons why female participation numbers are typically below those of males. [3]

3. Calculate the percentage difference in participation between males and females. Use the data provided in **Figure 2**. [1]

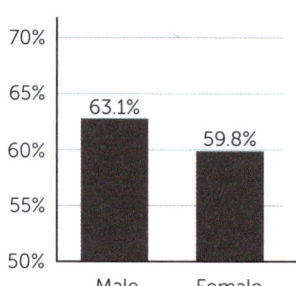

Figure 2: Sport England, November 2021.

Percentage of adults taking part in regular moderate exercise

Male: 63.1%
Female: 59.8%

2. Females are less likely to take part in competitive sport.[1] Some sports are stereotypically more male oriented e.g. boxing.[1] Less funding / sponsorship available for females.[1] Discrimination / sexism in some sports[1] (even though there are very few sports clubs left that are formally males only). Lack of female role models / less media coverage of female sports people.[1] Pregnancy / menstruation may prevent participation.[1] Childcare may be difficult to find in order to create time for sport.[1] Lack of female sports clubs / teams locally.[1]

3. 63.1 − 59.8 = 3.3%.[1]

As of 2022, the UK Chief Medical Officers' Guidelines recommend that adults should get at least 150 minutes of moderate physical activity per week. Children and young people aged 5–18 should aim to do 60 minutes of activity each day.

Moderate activity means something that raises the heart and breathing rate. This includes walking, cycling and PE classes.

Social grouping by Ethnicity, religion and culture

Examples of factors affecting participation:

Religion and culture

Certain religions require specific clothing or commitments that may make participation harder to achieve, for example **fasting**.

Role models

There may be a lack of cultural role models for others to aspire to.

Access

It may be perceived that not all activities are inclusive for those from different cultural backgrounds.

Discrimination

Racism by other sportspeople or spectators can affect people's decision to participate in a sport, and can negatively influence a team coach's decisions. Some religious discrimination may prevent performers from wearing a hijab, or finding swimming hats to accommodate natural black hair, for example. **Homophobia** or **transphobia** may also negatively impact participation in sport.

Most of the factors that affect participation can be related to any of the social groups.

For example: more media coverage, an increase in positive role models, improved education or an increase in leisure time can all positively affect the participation rates of all of the social groups.

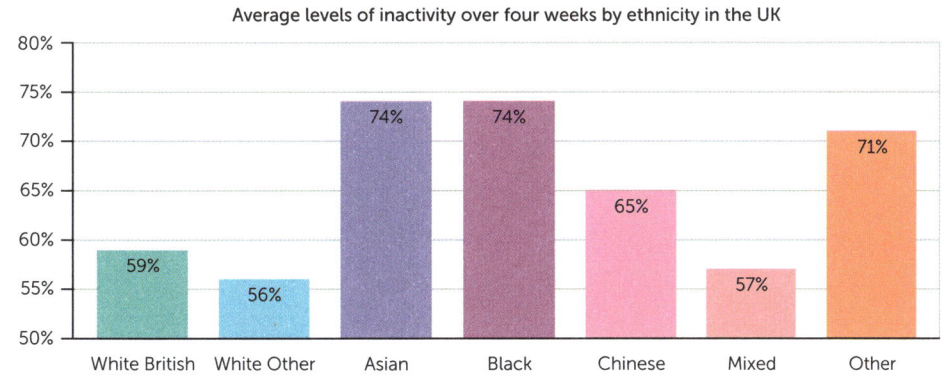

Figure 3: Sport England, November 2021

4. Identify **one** ethnicity group with the greatest levels of inactivity. [1]

   4. One from: Asian / black. [1]

Social grouping by Socio-economic group

People in society can be divided into various socio-economic groups according to their occupation, status, income and industry.

Those in higher socio-economic groups are more likely to be able to afford more expensive sports such as skiing, golf and polo.

5. Give **one** reason why activities such as running and general fitness classes tend to have a higher participation rate than showjumping or snowboarding. [1]

    5. Running and fitness classes have relatively low barriers to entry such as cost / skill level / equipment required.[1] The greatest proportion of society are in the lower socio-economic groups who may lean more towards sports that are less expensive to take part in.[1]

Social grouping by Disability

Examples of factors affecting participation:

Role models
There may be a lack of disabled role models to inspire disabled performers.

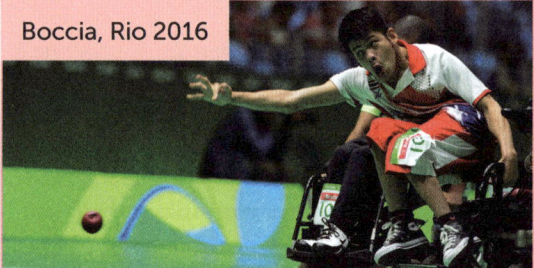

Boccia, Rio 2016

Discrimination
Some performers may feel that there is a negative **stereotype** towards those with a disability.

Media coverage
Despite increased media coverage of para sports, it is still a small fraction compared to that of mainstream sports.

Access
Some facilities may not have suitable access for wheelchair users.

Participation in sport by those with a disability is around 20% lower than that of able-bodied adults.

6. Explain how **two** named factors can negatively affect the participation rate of people with a disability. [4]

    6. Any two named factors with explanation: Factor: access[1] as some sports facilities do not cater for the accessibility requirements of all disabilities.[1] Factor: role models.[1] When there are only a few disabled role models, they are less able to act as an inspiration for other people with a disability to take part.[1] Factor: accessibility.[1] Some facilities may not be accessible for some disabled users.[1] Factor: stereotyping.[1] There may be a stereotype that disabled users are unable to participate.[1]

3.2.1

COMMERCIALISATION, THE MEDIA AND SPORT

Commercialisation is to manage or to exploit (an organisation or activity) in a way designed to make profit. This involves **sponsorship** and **media** coverage.

The golden triangle

The **golden triangle** is a term used to show the links and relationship between **sponsorship**, **sport** and the **media**.

Each of the three aspects in the golden triangle are reliant on each other.

1.  The media (usually television) pays money to the sport to be able to film and broadcast the event(s).

2.  The media, for example Sky Sports, Amazon Prime or BT Sport, provides sports coverage to gain revenue from viewer subscriptions.

3.  Companies pay money to the sport to sponsor an event.

4.  Sporting organisations receive valuable funding and income from sponsors and the media which can be invested in areas such as grass roots sport, stadia or elite athlete development.

5.  By sponsoring the event, sponsors increase their publicity and brand awareness which they hope will boost sales of their products and services, increasing their profit by more than the cost of sponsorship.

---

1. Explain the relationship between sport, media and sponsorship. [3]
2. Using a practical example from physical activity and sport, explain **one** way in which commercialisation can have a negative impact. [2]

   1. Any three from: Sport receives money from sponsors and from the media.[1] Sponsors can showcase their brand to increase their profit via the media.[1] The media gain money from subscribers who want to watch the sport on television.[1]

   2. External funding can be relied upon and withdrawn at a moment's notice as they do not want to be associated with poor performance, injury or misbehaviour.[1] Anthony Joshua lost sponsorship when he lost his world heavyweight title.[1]

      Minority sports / groups rarely attract enough attention to engage major sponsorship as the sponsors want large audiences[1] which means these sports continue to struggle in terms of their own funding and promotion. Women's football clubs are paid only a fraction by their sponsors in comparison to men's clubs.[1]

ADVANTAGES AND DISADVANTAGES OF COMMERCIALISATION AND THE MEDIA

Sponsorship influences the commercialisation of physical activity and sport through a variety of ways.

Positive and negative impacts

Performer

A golfer sponsored by Nike.

- ➕ **Clothing and equipment:** Performers receive free or subsidised clothing and equipment to wear from the sponsor. This will also be of the highest quality which can provide an advantage.
- ➕ **Profile:** Coverage in the media can bring fame and allow performers to ask for more money. They may also get the chance to earn from product endorsements. Performers can use a high profile to raise awareness of wider issues and campaigns to champion change for good.
- ➖ **Media and sponsor demands:** Media may dictate when events take place which can lead to burn out and increased injury over a long season. Sponsors may require players to attend sponsorship events which may conflict with training schedules.
- ➖ **Reputation damage:** A poor decision, act of aggression or insensitive comment can lead to negative press, a loss of privacy and loss of sponsorship.
- ➖ **Pressure:** Media increases the pressure to perform and can demand interviews, which can reduce enjoyment. Pressure can also instigate the 'win at all costs' mindset which can lead to deviance or cheating.

Sport

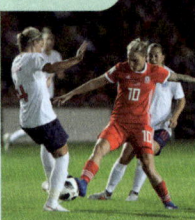

Women's football Wales v England, World Cup Qualifier.

- ➕ **Interest:** Interest and participation in the sport will grow because of media coverage / more role models are created.
- ➕ **Competitions:** There may be more competitions held.
- ➕ **Income:** The sport will earn more money from sponsorship and media coverage. This money can be spent on grass roots sport, larger prize pots, coaching, development, and facilities.
- ➕ **Education:** Media coverage will inform the public about the sport.
- ➕ **Facilities:** Better or bigger facilities can be built.
- ➖ **Scandals:** Reputational damage if scandals are publicised in the media, e.g. match fixing.
- ➖ **Attachment:** Sport may get attached to an undesirable brand / sponsor.
- ➖ **Reliance:** The sport may become too reliant on sponsor / media money.
- ➖ **Start times:** Start times maybe dictated by the media.
- ➖ **Appropriateness:** Some sponsors may be promoting an unhealthy lifestyle through gambling, fast food, vaping or alcohol for example.

Some points can be expressed as positives OR as negatives. For example, an increased profile in the media may be what the performer hopes for or they may see it as adding to their pressure.

Positive and negative impacts continued

Audience / spectator

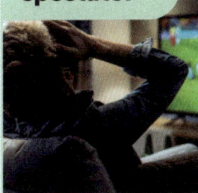

Home viewing of sport.

- ➕ **24/7 coverage:** Spectators can gain access to 24/7 news and coverage through the media.
- ➕ **Education:** Spectators can be educated through media channels.
- ➕ **Better viewing experience:** Action replays / slow-motion.
- ➖ **Traditional nature:** Loss of the traditional nature of the sport- e.g., start times being changed to suit the media.
- ➖ **Adverts:** Viewing experience may be interrupted by sponsors' adverts.
- ➖ **Tickets:** Tickets can be difficult to obtain and expensive when they are available owing to an increase in popularity.
- ➖ **Merchandise:** Sponsors may drive up the cost of merchandise.
- ➖ **Subscriptions:** Viewers may have to pay to watch televised sport.

Sponsors

Corporate hospitality boxes.

- ➕ **Profit:** Increased profit due to brand exposure and better sales.
- ➕ **Client experience:** Gain free tickets to entertain clients at events.
- ➕ **Taxation:** Sponsorship can be used to reduce the sponsor's tax bill.
- ➖ **Reputation:** Impacted by negative publicity if a scandal happens in the associated sport or performer that they sponsor. A poorly performing sports team may also cast a poor light on the sponsor.
- ➖ **Cost:** Sponsorship can be very expensive and the sponsor may be legally tied in to continue sponsorship for a period.
- ➖ **Supply and demand:** If demand for products or services increases significantly, the company may find it hard to supply everyone.

Justify why sponsorship and media coverage can be positive for sports performers. [3]

Any three from: Access to state-of-the-art equipment which can enhance performance.[1] Provision of free and/or performance-enhancing clothing.[1] Use of high-quality facilities to train at.[1] Higher profile within the media, giving access to product endorsement / further sponsorship / more money.[1]

⭐ Be careful to focus on two things when answering questions about this topic:

Firstly, which group is being asked about e.g., spectators, and secondly, is the examiner asking for positives, negatives or for both? It is common for students to write their answers about only the positive effects on performers even when the question is not asking for that.

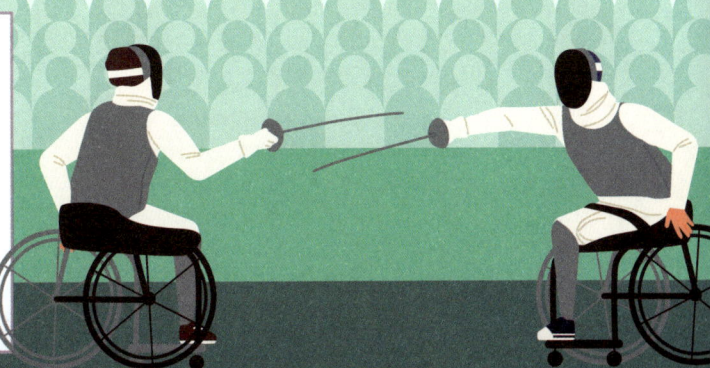

TYPES OF SPORTING BEHAVIOUR

Sport should be played in the manner it is intended. Bending or breaking the rules can have serious consequences for performers and the reputation of their sport.

Sportsmanship

Sportsmanship means **fair play**. It is ethical, appropriate, polite and fair behaviour while participating in a game or athletic event.

Performers who show good sportsmanship will:
- Follow the rules. Avoid cheating, foul play or aggression.
- Respect the opposition. Be friendly to all competitors and avoid unpleasantness.
- Take measures to reduce the risk of injury to others. Help injured players before playing on.
- Promote their sport in a positive way and be a positive role model.
- Be gracious in victory and defeat. Accept the decision of umpires, referees and officials.

Ethics is a set of moral principles based on what is deemed right and wrong, not simply what is legal or illegal.

Gamesmanship

Gamesmanship means pushing or bending the rules to gain unfair advantage.
The laws of a sport may be interpreted in ways, which whilst not illegal, are not in the spirit of the game. Coaches can also be guilty of encouraging such behaviour.

Examples of gamesmanship include:
- Football players wasting time with the ball in anticipation of the final whistle.
- Basketball players holding their opponent.
- Tennis players deliberately calling 'out' when the ball was 'in'.
- Runners pushing another competitor.
- Golfer coughing to distract an opponent in a putt.
- Rugby players moving the penalty spot closer to the posts.
- Cricket bowlers sledging a batter to intimidate them.

Deviance

Deviance means behaviour that is either immoral or seriously breaks the rules and norms of a sport.

Deviance and gamesmanship have a fine line between them, but they both tend to happen when sports people place too high a priority or importance on winning over anything else.

Deviance includes **cheating**, **violence**, taking **performance enhancing drugs** and **match fixing**. Deviancy damages the reputation of sports and could result in a loss of income or sponsorship. Popularity and participation may fall, and with that, income from ticket sales and media rights. Fewer young people may take up the sport, reducing the pool of new talent.

Give **one** reason for gamesmanship in sport. [1]

To increase the likelihood of winning / to turn the game around if losing.[1] To gain fame / financial reward for winning.[1] To feel clever by 'playing' the rules to the letter.[1] Copying the behaviour of others.[1] Frustration of losing a point / being in a losing position.[1] Orders from the coach.[1]

Reasons for and consequences of player deviance

Lack of moral code

A **lack of positive education** as young players and **pressure to win** can cause some players to resort to cheating.

In 2018, the captain and vice-captain of the Australia cricket team were found guilty of illegally tampering with the ball by using sandpaper to rough up the edges to change its course through the air. They received 12-month bans, lost the respect of their peers and brought Australian cricket into disrepute. Team sponsors cancelled their contracts and a large media deal fell through as a result.

Copying others

Many performers copy poor technique from older colleagues who may have a lack of moral code themselves. However, during the 1990s, there was culture of greater acceptance to some degree of deviance or violence in football.

In an extreme example in 2008, Taylor tackled da Silva so hard it broke his leg in four places.

Financial pressure

The income and media attention associated with success can drive sports people at all levels to dirty tactics.

Juventus match officials and several referees were found to be at the heart of the 'calciopoli' match fixing scandal in 2006. As a consequence, they lost the trust of their fans and lost credibility in the sport. Juventus were stripped of their league title and relegated. The club and those directly involved faced significant fines and potential jail sentences.

'Win at all costs' mentality

Some performers will do anything at any cost to win. **Coaches** can also impose great pressure on performers.

In 1994, Tonya Harding won her ice-skating championship after her main rival was attacked with a baton, putting her out of the competition. Harding and accomplices were later convicted with related charges. Harding was banned for life.

Stress of the situation

In the heat of the moment, performers can take any opportunity to bring down others to improve their own outcome. Especially if there is a perception of lenient punishment compared to the potential upside of their actions.

Schumacher appeared to turn in aggressively against Hill in the last race of the 1994 F1 Championship, ultimately putting both cars out of the race and handing himself a win by one point.

EXAMINATION PRACTICE

For questions 1 and 2, use the information in Figure 1 to decide if A, B, C or D is correct.

Figure 1 shows an approximate popularity of different sports and activities.

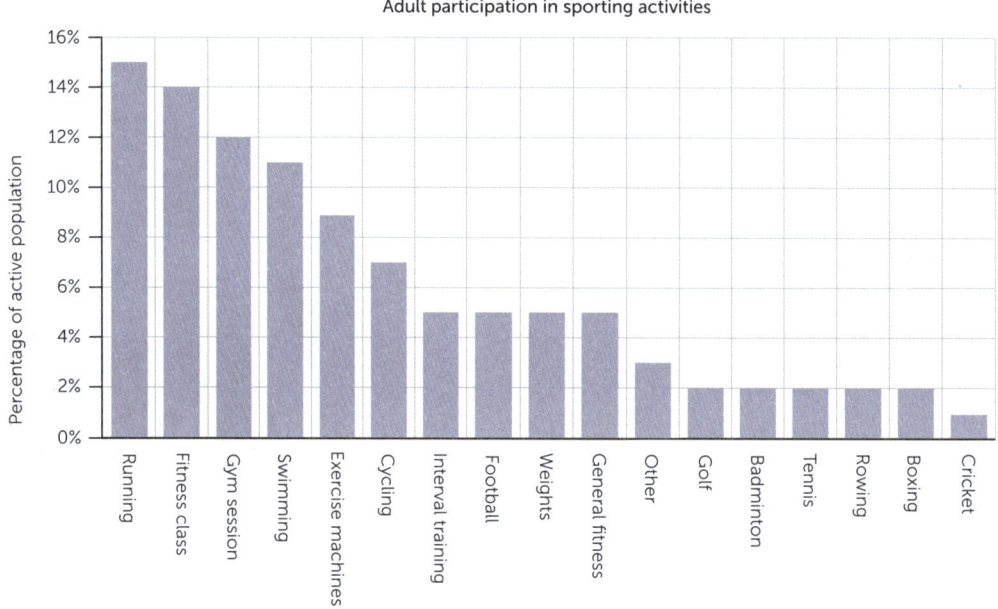

Figure 1

1. Identify the sport with the greatest participation rate. [1]
   A – Cricket
   B – Cycling
   C – Football
   D – Running

2. Which **one** of the following sports or activities has the same participation rate as golf? [1]
   A – Badminton
   B – Fitness classes
   C – Football
   D – Interval training

3. Participation in sport by those with a disability is around 20% lower than that of able-bodied adults. Evaluate the impact of **three** different factors in encouraging an increase in participation for disabled performers. [9]

4. Suggest why the percentage of active adults typically increases between March and October each year. [1]

5. Identify **two** social groups that have typically lower levels of participation in sport compared to the national averages. [2]

6. The charts in **Figure 2** and **Figure 3** show the levels of disposable income and the levels of physical activity across the UK.

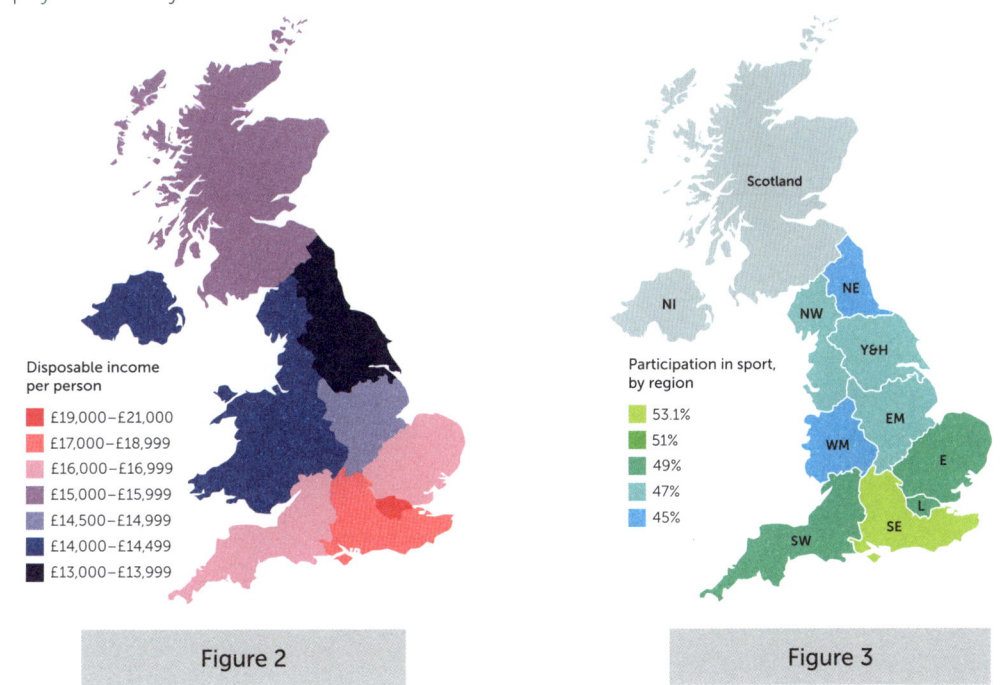

Figure 2

Figure 3

(a) From the information provided in Figures 2 and 3, Explain the relationship between disposable income and levels of activity. [1]
(b) Estimate the level of activity in Scotland as a percentage. [1]
(c) Calculate the percentage difference between the most and least active areas of the UK. [1]
(d) Analyse **two** ways that local authorities can increase the level of participation in sports by adults living in the region. [6]

7. **Figure 4** explains the rising trend in annual income for the English Premier League clubs over a decade.

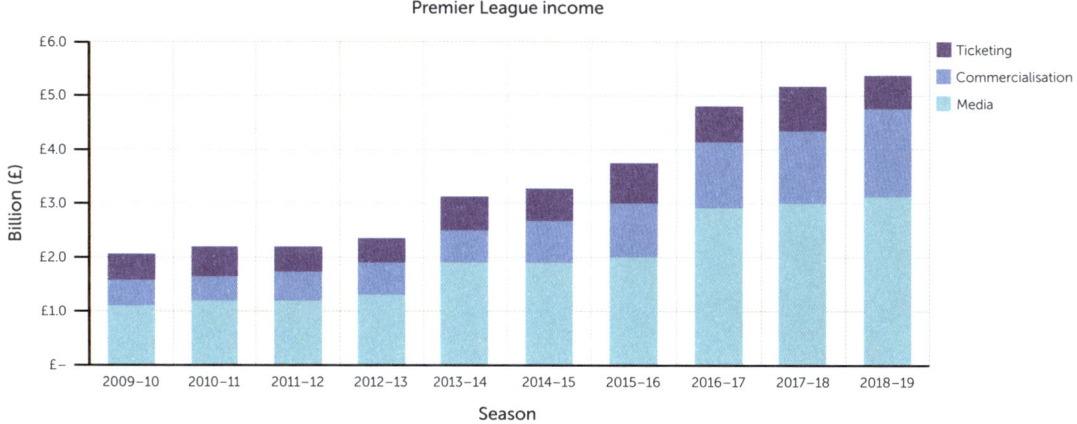

Figure 4

(a) Revenues jumped significantly in 2016–17. State the primary source of the rise in income. [1]

(b) Evaluate the impact that the media has had on sport. [9]

THE USE OF DATA

Specification coverage

The use of data analysis skills are spread across the components and topics.

Requirements

Demonstrate an understanding of how data is collected – both qualitative and quantitative

Present data, including graphs and tables.

Analyse and evaluate data, including graphs and tables.

UNDERSTANDING HOW DATA IS COLLECTED

The collection of data is crucial to analysis and the formation of conclusions. How data is collected often depends on the type of data that is required.

Quantitative data

Quantitative data is objective information which can be defined without opinion. It deals with numbers for example a score, distance, time or level. For this reason, it is more easily statistically analysed. Methods for collecting quantitative data commonly include **questionnaires** and **surveys**.

In a survey of 100 members of a local sports club, a questionnaire asked for the number of hours of exercise that respondents undertook each week. It also asked for their resting heart rate. Question 1 was segmented by hour to allow for easier analysis.

1. In the average week, how many hours of vigorous exercise do you complete?

| 0 | 1 | 2 | ③ | 4 | 5 | 6 | 7 | 8 | 9+ |

2. After a period of 20 mins after exercise, what is your resting heart rate in BPM?

64

Qualitative data

Qualitative data involves subjective information and deals with descriptions. This includes opinions and emotions. **Interviews** and **observations** allow for more detailed and descriptive responses.

Whilst conducting the same survey, interviews with some members collected the following response to exercise patterns:

> "I love running on cold mornings, but I tend not to bother if it is raining."

Observations can be used to judge human behaviour over time to find patterns. The manager of the sports club observed that sports club members tended to change their use over time.

> "A lot of people have high levels of exercise in January but that quickly tails off until the summer when longer evenings bring more people outside."

PRESENTING DATA

Data can be presented in graphical formats to show patterns more clearly.

Presenting data in tables

The data collected from the sports club survey can be tallied and averaged in a **table**:

Exercise hours per week	Frequency	Average resting heart rate
0	3	78
1	16	75
2	24	72
3	17	68
4	12	69
5	10	66
6	8	65
7	3	63
8	5	61
9	2	57

24 people exercised for 2 hours per week

Plotting basic bar charts and line graphs

Using the data in the table above, a **bar chart** (figure 1) can be plotted to show the number of people that exercise for 0–9 hours per week. A **line graph** (figure 2) can be plotted to show the average heart rate for club members for each level of exercise.

Figure 1: Bar chart

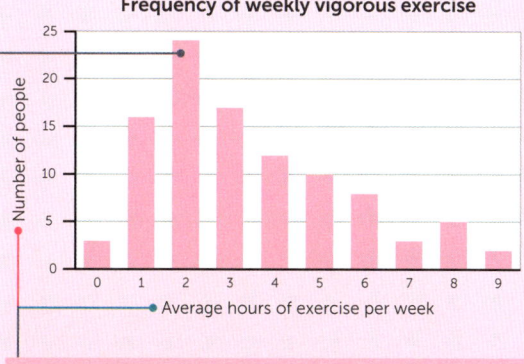

Figure 2: Line graph

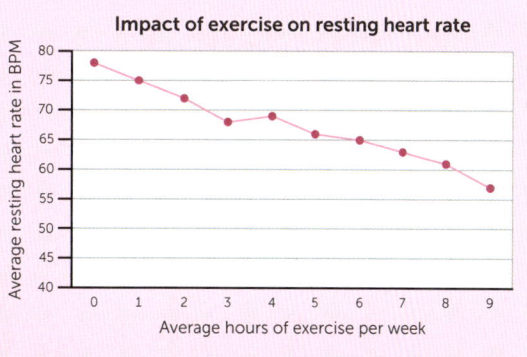

Always label the **x** and **y** axes on charts and graphs for full marks. Axis labels should include the units, for example: people, BPM or weeks.

Mark each point on a line graph, then join the markers.

Look at the line graph in Figure 2. Suggest the relationship between resting heart rate and hours of exercise in this sample of people. [1]

Those who did greater amounts of weekly exercise had lower resting heart rates.[1]

Edexcel GCSE **Physical Education** – The use of data

ANALYSIS AND EVALUATION OF DATA

Once data has been collected, it can be analysed, graphed and then interpreted. An evaluation of the data can more easily be made after this process.

Interpreting tabular data

The data in the table below shows the number of medals won by the GBR team in the Summer Olympics since 1992. Without some analysis, data tables can be difficult to interpret.

Medals	Barcelona 1992	Atlanta 1996	Sydney 2000	Athens 2004	Beijing 2008	London 2012	Rio 2016	Tokyo 2021
Gold	5	1	11	9	19	29	27	22
Silver	3	8	10	9	13	18	23	20
Bronze	12	6	7	12	19	18	17	22

This data could be analysed, for example, by sorting or by finding the totals for each year:

Total	20	15	28	30	51	65	67	64

Figure 1: GBR Summer Olympic medals since 1992

1. From the table of data presented in Figure 1, identify the most successful year for the GBR team in terms of gold medals won. [1]

   2012.[1]

Interpreting graphical data

Bar charts

Data presented graphically is often clearer and easier to extract useful information from.

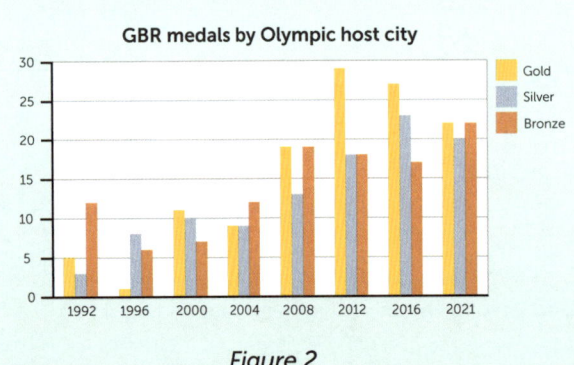

Figure 2

2. Look at the bar chart presented in Figure 2. Suggest **two** possible reasons why the performance of GBR athletes improved after 1996. [2]

   (National Lottery) funding was diverted into elite sport in 1996.[1] *A new high-performance system spread across UK sports, putting the concept of marginal gains at the heart of training.*[1] *New, raw talent was better nurtured.*[1] *Team spirit increased in Beijing 2008 and the winning feeling has increased confidence and pride in athletes and their performance directors.*[1]

Interpreting graphical data continued

Line graphs

Line graphs are often useful to see **trends** within the data. A trendline can also be added.

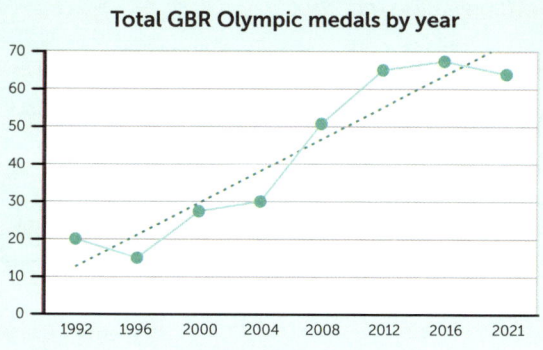

Figure 3

3. From the line graph presented in Figure 3, suggest the number of GBR medals likely in 2024.
Give a reason for your estimate. [2]

60–70[1] medals based on a plateau since 2012.[1] / 70–85[1] based on the trend line.[1]

Pie charts

Pie charts are used to show the proportions of a whole. In analysing charts, it is often helpful to look for **patterns**, **similarities** and **differences** by **comparing** sets of information. For example, two data points on a graph could be compared, or two points in time.

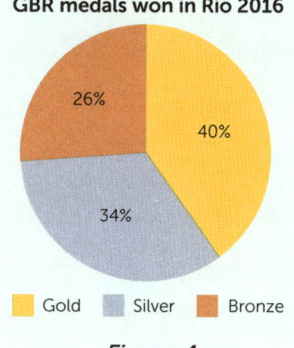

Figure 4

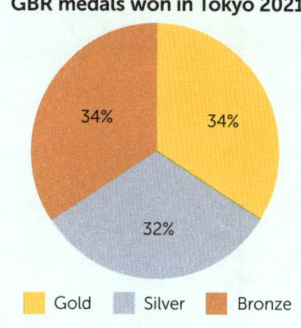

Figure 5

4. Look at Figures 4 and 5. Analyse the performance of the GBR team in both years. [2]

The proportion of silver medals remained at roughly a third.[1] Bronze medals increased in 2021 whilst gold medals decreased / potential gold or silver medallists may have lost out to gain a silver or bronze instead.[1] Performance was roughly consistent from one year to the next.[1]

 Make comparisons where possible and draw conclusions from data using the information provided and your own knowledge.

Edexcel GCSE **Physical Education** – **The use of data**

The use of data

EXAMINATION PRACTICE

1. Which **one** of the following is an example of qualitative data? [1]
   - ☐ A – The Austrian skier has won five previous world champion slalom events
   - ☐ B – His split time was slower in the middle section by +0.42
   - ☐ C – The Austrian skier looks uncomfortable at the moment
   - ☐ D – He placed fourth in this race

2. **Figure 1** shows a table containing the number of yellow cards handed out over six seasons for Windham Athletic football team.

Season	2017/18	2018/19	2019/20	2020/21	2021/22	2022/23
Yellow cards	58	71	49	44	42	41

   Figure 1

   (a) Draw a bar chart using the graph paper below and the data provided in **Figure 1**. [2]

   Interpret the data in **Figure 1**.
   - (b) Identify **one** piece of outlying or anomalous data from the series. [1]
   - (c) Identify the trend shown in the data. [1]
   - (d) Suggest **two** reasons for the trend. [2]
   - (e) Suggest what the number of yellow cards is likely to be for the 2023/24 season. [1]

112 ClearRevise

NON-EXAM ASSESSMENT (NEA)
Practical performance and PEP

Information about the non-examined assessment:

Assessed by teachers
125 marks
40% of the qualification grade

Component 3: Practical performance — 30% of the total GCSE: 105 marks

The three activities that you choose must come from the lists below and should include:
- A team activity,
- An individual activity, **and**
- Any other activity of your choice

Team sports:
Acrobatic gymnastics, association football, badminton, basketball, camogie, cricket, dance, figure skating, futsal, Gaelic football, handball, hockey, hurling, ice hockey, inline roller hockey, lacrosse, netball, rowing, rugby league, rugby union, sailing, sculling, squash, table tennis, tennis, volleyball, water polo.

Specialist sports: blind cricket, goalball, powerchair football, table cricket, wheelchair basketball, wheelchair rugby.

Individual sports:
Amateur boxing, athletics, badminton, canoeing / kayaking (slalom or sprint), cycling, dance, diving, equestrian, figure skating, golf, gymnastics, rock climbing, sailing, sculling, skiing, snowboarding, squash, swimming, table tennis, tennis, trampoline, windsurfing.

Specialist sports: Boccia, polybat.

Component 4: Personal Exercise Programme (PEP) — 10% of the total GCSE: 20 marks

Component 3

PRACTICAL PERFORMANCE

Your non-examined assessment requires you to take part in **three** different activities. For each activity, you should evidence specific skills and your performance in conditioned practices and in the full context of the sport.

Skills in isolation

Each of the activities have a list of **skills** and **techniques in isolation**.

In most activities you will need to complete 4 of the 5 listed skills although in some activities like cricket, you are required to complete all the listed skills for your position.

You are assessed in your ability to perform each skill with accuracy, control and fluency. Assessment incorporates the preparation to perform, the exertion of and the recovery process for each skill.

Look at the relevant page in the practical performance assessment criteria booklet for more detail relevant to your chosen activity.

Performance in conditioned practices and in the full context

You are expected to demonstrate application of the skills, techniques and decision making required whilst under pressure in conditioned situations and in the full formal version of the sport.

Be aware that:

- In team games, you would normally be seen in the full sided version but for moderation it can be in a slightly lower number in each team (as per NGB guidelines).
- You should demonstrate a range of skills.
- Your physical attributes e.g., components of fitness will form part of the assessment.
- You must demonstrate suitable decision making and problem solving in the competitive context.
- You should select and apply suitable tactics with the aim of outwitting others.
- You should have appropriate knowledge of the rules and regulations when performing in the competitive context.

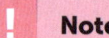 **Note**

Moderation can occur live if your centre has 15 or more candidates. Live moderation will be filmed by the teachers in the centre. If external video evidence is being used (for example if your centre has 14 or fewer candidates) this evidence should fully meet the criteria and be uploaded onto Edexcel's digital platform.

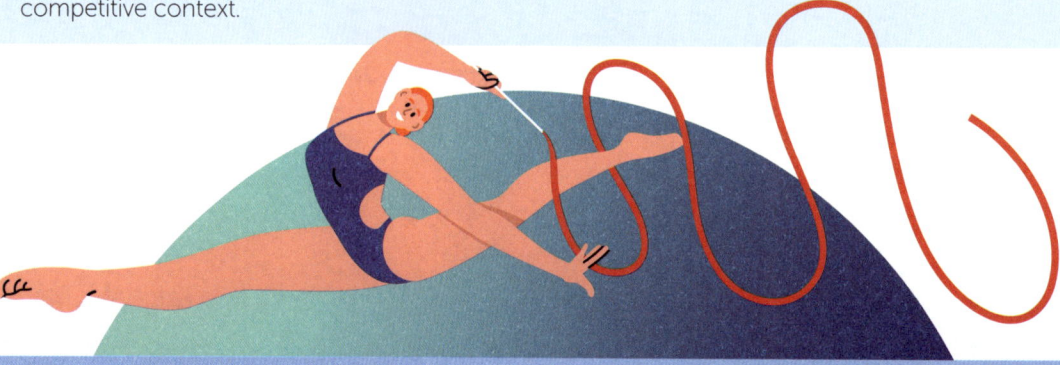

Component 4

PERSONAL EXERCISE PROGRAMME (PEP)

Having completed three practical performances, you are also required to complete a Personal Exercise Programme (PEP).

You can write your PEP on one of your three activities, but you could decide to write it on another activity if you wish, as long as it is an activity that is included in the specification.

The PEP has three main parts:
- Aim and planning analysis
- Carrying out and monitoring the PEP
- Evaluation of fitness data and programme

> You can write a very successful PEP based on improving one component of fitness and one aspect of practical performance.

1 Aim and planning analysis

In this section you will:
- Complete a **PARQ** (physical activity readiness questionnaire).
- Select **one** component of fitness and **one** method of training (you can choose more if you feel it would help to achieve your goals).
- Collect data and identify an aspect of performance that you hope to improve as a result of gaining specific fitness.
- Analyse your pre-training fitness test results to justify why you have chosen to improve your given goals.
- Include **SMART** targets to achieve as part of the PEP.

2 Carrying out and monitoring the PEP

In this section you will:
- Carry out and monitor training over a 6-8 week period.
- Implement appropriate principles of training to ensure that the goals are met.
- Record every training session.
- Gather data as appropriate.
- Note and justify any modifications to your original plan.

Note

Note: There is a template to record training sessions on the Pearson Edexcel website.

3 Evaluation of fitness data and programme

In this section you will:
- Evaluate the success or otherwise of the programme.
- Compare pre-training data with data gathered throughout the programme.
- Use the data to justify why performance levels have increased (or not).
- Make recommendations for further improvements and suggest ways to optimise future performance.
- Compare data in a graphical format with an accompanying explanation.

EXAMINATION PRACTICE ANSWERS

Paper 1, Topic 1

1. A – Femur. [1]
2. D – The movement of the arm away from the midline of the body. [1]
3. B – Cervical. [1]
4. C – Increased heart rate. [1]
5. A – Left atrium → left ventricle → right atrium → right ventricle. [1]
6. (a) Blood clotting / healing a wound. [1]
   (b) Oxygen. [1]
7. Support [1], protection of vital organs by flat bones [1], movement [1], to provide a structural shape [1], provide points for muscular attachment [1], for mineral storage [1] and blood cell production. [1] [3]
8. Ligaments are less elastic than tendons. [1] Ligaments connect bone to bone / tendons connect bone to muscle. [1] Ligaments provide support and stability to a joint whereas tendons are designed to move the bone at a joint. [1] [2]
9. Tricep. [1]
10. Weight bearing / strong. [1] Spread the load / impact across the rest of the foot of a jump on take-off or landing / or strike as they run. [1] [2]
11. (a) [2]

Joint	Classification of joint	Range of movement possible
Neck (A)	Pivot [1]	Rotation [1]
Wrist (B)	Condyloid [1]	Flexion to extension [1] / Abduction and adduction [1]

   (b) Protection of the brain [1] in a header.[1] [2]
   (c) Voluntary muscles require conscious thought and effort [1] which enables the player to adjust their throwing action appropriately [1] to suit the context.[1] [2]
   (d) Type IIx fibres are used for short, powerful bursts of movement. [1] Type IIx fibres provide the most powerful contractions to throw the ball with force / or to jump to gain height. [1] Type IIx fibres are essential to be able to make a powerful throw / throw over a greater distance to a team player that has less chance of being defended. [1] [3]
12. (a) Muscles are attached to bones by tendons. [1] When muscles contract, they pull on the tendon, which moves the bone. [1] Muscles work in antagonistic pairs. [1] As one contracts, the other relaxes. [1] Bones create lever systems which can be moved. [1] [3]
    (b) Tidal volume shows the change in lung volume during a normal breath, in or out. [1]
    (c) It increases. [1]
    (d) Adrenaline may have caused it to increase. [1] A quick warm up on the side lines may have caused it to increase. [1] [1]
    (e) Intercostal muscles. [1] Sternocleidomastoid muscle. [1] [1]
    (f) Alveoli provide a large surface area for gas exchange to take place. [1] Walls are only one cell thick so gas molecules have a short distance to travel. [1] Oxygen moves from a higher concentration in the alveoli to the blood in the capillaries. [1] Carbon dioxide moves from the capillaries into the alveoli and into the lungs to be exhaled. [1] [3]
    (g) Can play basketball for longer / move around the court more without getting tired. [1] Can play at a higher intensity for longer without getting tired. [1] [1]
    (h) Carbohydrates. Allow glucose/glycogen. [1]

Paper 1, Topic 2

1. C – Third class lever. [1]
2. D – The load in between the effort and the fulcrum. [1]
3. (a) Plane – Sagittal. [1] Axis – Frontal. [1] [2]
   (b) Class 2 lever. [1]
   (c) Diagram must be labelled. Accept load/resistance. [1] [2]

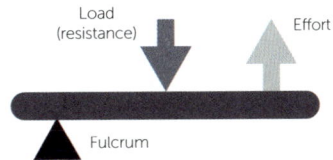

   (d) In third class levers, the effort arm is always shorter than resistance arm. / It has a short effort arm. / MA = effort arm / resistance (load). [1] Lever has low strength to effort ratio. [1] Lever is inefficient when considering strength. [1] 3rd class levers allow a load to be moved more quickly / over a greater distance. [1] Third class levers always have an MA of less than 1. [1] [2]

Paper 1, Topic 3

1. D – Decision making. [1]
2. B – Motor racing. [1]
3. B – Progressive overload. [1]
4. C – Cooper 12-minute run/walk test and the Harvard step test. [1]
5. B – 204. [1]
6. (a) A – Anabolic steroids. [1]
   (b) Two from: Improve concentration [1], suppress fatigue [1], releases protected reserves of energy [1], raise confidence levels [1], increase aggression. [1] [2]
7. (a) Power is explosive strength / the product of strength × speed. [1]
   (b) Examples include: Sprinting to launch out of the blocks and sustain speed / hurdles / boxing to throw a fast, hard punch / shot put to launch the put / volleyball to spike. [1]
   (c) Standing vertical jump test. [1]
8. (a) Flexibility. [1] Increases muscular elasticity which reduces chance of injury / decreases muscle soreness. [1] Limbs have a greater range of movement so they can reach more shots / improve their technique. [1] Flexibility improves balance and mobility, keeping the player responsive / on their feet. [1]
   Cardiovascular endurance. [1] Increases the duration that they are able to perform at their peak for with a raised heart rate. [1]
   Muscular endurance. [1] Avoids fatigue in muscles used repeatedly throughout a match. [1]
   Speed. [1] Helps a player to reach shots on the other side of the court / aids position between shots to return to the centre of the court. [1] [2]
   (b) Definition, 1 mark: The ability to move two or more body parts together smoothly and efficiently. [1]
   Importance, up to 2 marks: Hand eye coordination is required when hitting the ball. [1]
   The player must align their body with the incoming shot and position themself to strike with power. [1]
   The racket should hit the ball in the sweet spot so that they get maximum power on the ball. [1]
   To hit a ball on the move. [1]
   The player must move into the right position on the court to hit the ball before the ball reaches that point. [1]
   Better coordination should result in more points awarded / fewer unforced errors, providing a competitive advantage. [1]
   A serve must be coordinated to throw the ball up and hit it perfectly. [1] [3]
9. David's score indicates that he has average agility. [1]
   Elizabeth's score indicates that she has good agility. [1]
   Even though David performed the test faster than Elizabeth, as a male, he is expected to be faster [1] /
   the scores compensate for males and females so Elizabeth is grouped in a higher performance category. [1] [3]

Edexcel GCSE **Physical Education – Answers**

10. (a) Use the handgrip dynamometer in the dominant hand. [1] Squeeze the handle with maximum effort. [1] Keep the elbow at 90 degrees. [1] Keep the arm close to the body. [1] Record the best score. [1] [3]
    (b) This question should be marked in accordance with the levels-based mark scheme on **page 123**. [6]
    Indicative content may include:

    ### Knowledge of the grip test e.g:
    - The test measures grip strength.
    - The test does not measure the strength of any other muscle group.

    ### Application to a rock climber and a kayaker e.g:
    - A rock climber needs strong hands and grip in order to hold on to a rock face.
    - A kayaker does not need a very strong grip, other than to hold onto the paddle.
    - The test is a standard test to measure grip strength with national benchmarks.

    ### The importance of the test to a rock climber and a kayaker e.g:
    - Grip strength is a fundamental skill for rock climbing as climbers need to use hand holds.
    - A kayaker needs to be able to hold on to the paddle, but there are far more important muscle groups such as the arms and back that depend more on strength in kayaking.
    - The test does, to some extent, replicate the movements of a rock climber using hand holds. It does not replicate the movements of kayaking.
    - Grip strength dynamometers may measure grip more in the whole hand rather than just the strength of the fingertips to cling onto a rock, so it may be limited as a measure of climbing ability.
    - Grip strength is a poor indicator of ability for a kayaker since it does not evaluate their overall strength, but it may provide some indication of general fitness and strength.
    - There are other standardised tests that may be better for both rock climbers and kayakers such as a sit-up bleep test or a wall toss test to measure muscular endurance and coordination.

11. (a) Three from: Avoid over training [1], wear appropriate clothing and footwear [1], use PPE [1], compete at the appropriate level [1], use the correct technique [1], lift and carry equipment safely [1], cool down properly [1]. [3]
    (b) This question should be marked in accordance with the levels-based mark scheme on **page 123**. [6]
    Indicative content may include:

    ### Knowledge of plyometric training and other factors e.g.
    - Plyometric training involves jumping, bounding and hopping
    - It is good at developing power / explosive strength, but also speed
    - Training involves creating an eccentric contraction of a muscle which moves straight into a larger concentric contraction to maximise the length of the contraction and the power of the muscle movement
    - Diet may improve performance alongside any types of training
    - The principles of training and FITT should be applied, regardless of the type of training
    - Callum should plan his warm-ups, rest periods and recovery.

    ### Application to Callum e.g.
    - Plyometric training can improve Callum's muscular endurance
    - Plyometric training can improve Callum's power
    - Plyometric training can improve Callum's speed
    - Power will be needed to avoid or quickly dodge an opponent
    - Callum will need a high level of fitness before starting plyometric training as it exerts high forces on muscles which could tear if he isn't already strong as there is a high risk of injury
    - If Callum adopts plyometric training during the football playing season, an injury could mean he misses the remaining fixtures
    - Callum would not need any specialist equipment and could practice plyometrics almost anywhere
    - He may need dietary supplements to increase his carbohydrate intake to convert this into glucose for energy, protein to help build and repair muscle (hypertrophy), fluids and salts for hydration and effective body function
    - SPORT and FITT need to be applied to ensure a safe and effective training program. Overload should be reached but not over done
    - Recovery practices should be put into place to reduce DOMS and prevent injury or tightness.

    ### Evaluation of the appropriateness of plyometrics and other factors to Callum e.g.
    - Plyometric training is well suited to improving speed and power in the legs which is a desirable attribute in a football player
    - Football players needs speed when running for/with the ball so increased leg power will improve this fitness component for Callum
    - Football players need explosive power in the legs to be able to respond to potential tackles, shoot or jump to head the ball so more powerful legs will help to improve the power and accuracy of a shot, improve height from a standing jump and improve the speed of response to avoid a tackle or fallen player.

- Training can be tailored to Callum to ensure that it is suitable for his current level of fitness and strength and that he has sufficient recovery time before the next match
- In a full match, other training methods may replicate the sporting movements of football more closely or provide greater benefits to Callum
- Callum could also combine plyometric training with other types of training to work on his cardiovascular (aerobic) endurance, core stability and agility such as interval training and circuit training to provide benefits of both aerobic and anaerobic exercise which reflects the stop/start nature of football and the bursts of energy required when a player prepares to get on the ball / gets the ball
- Ice baths, massages and a planned cool down routine including stretches will help reduce delayed onset muscle soreness (DOMS) and aid a faster recovery before the next match/training session
- Training should reflect the SPORT and FITT principles so that it is specific to Callum's needs, so that progress overload is reached and to avoid tedium.

Accept any other relevant points.

12. Warming up prepares your body for activity by raising heart rate / speeding up your cardiovascular system. [1] Increased blood flow loosens the joints [1] and provides greater flow of oxygen to the muscles. [1] Stretching prepares muscles for physical stress and improves the range of movement. [1] [2]

13. (i) Overuse injuries as the body is forced to work too hard, too quickly / has not been given time to recover since the last training session. [1]
    (ii) Scrum cap / helmet / shin pads / gloves / gum shield. [1]
    (iii) Concussion / bruising / chafing / blisters / damage to teeth. [1]

14. To review medical history / to predetermine any potential heart conditions that may make training unsafe. [1] To assess readiness for safe exercise. [1] To make recommendations for amendments to training or personal exercise programme (PEP) based on any health issues. [1] [1]

Paper 2, Topic 1

1. D – Reduced stress. [1]
2. B – Gradual decline. [1]
3. C – 2018. [1]
4. (a) Basic human needs are being met (food, shelter and clothing). The individual has friendship and support, some value in society, is socially active and has little stress in social circumstances. [1]
   (b) Two from: Opportunities to socialise with other people, [1] make friends, [1] enjoy some teamwork or team sports, [1] / cooperate with other people. [1] [2]
   (c) Improved mental health / self-esteem / appearance / reduced depression [1] could improve the desire to train or exercise (in public). [1] Improved blood pressure / diet / quitting smoking [1] could make exercise easier to approach / more enjoyable / more manageable. [1] Improved friendship groups / social standing / reduced loneliness [1] may provide greater desire / opportunities to train socially. [1] [2]

5. Baseline fitness data should be considered [1] so that the plan meets the right level of challenge for the student. [1] A PARQ [1] assessment should be conducted to ensure that the programme takes into account any underlying health issues. [1] The programme should be matched to the goals of the student [1] so that it can focus on the right components of fitness. [1] [2]

6. (a) 25–30%. [1]
   (b) Heart disease [1], high cholesterol [1], hypertension (high blood pressure caused by a narrowing of the arteries). [1] [1]
   (c) Consume fewer calories. [1] Increase energy expenditure. [1] [1]
   (d) Award one mark for points correctly plotted on the graph. One for correctly labelled axes. [2]

7. (a) Sustained exercise burns a lot of energy [1] which needs to be replaced through increased calorific intake. [1] Additional nutrients / protein / sugars are required [1] to help fuel the body / repair muscles. [1] 2500 calories a day for men is recommended [1] but this should be increased according to the additional levels of activity undertaken. [1] [2]

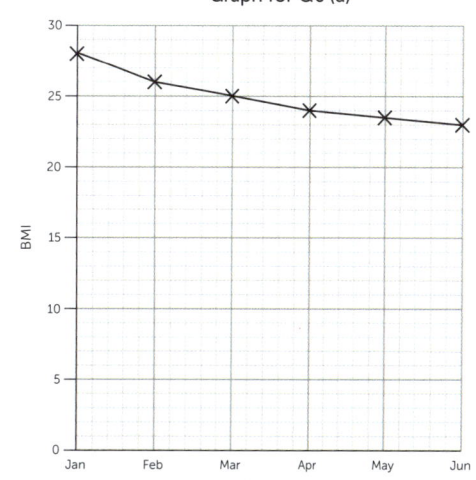

Graph for Q6 (d)

(b) Prehydration before starting each race day. [1] Carry water on the bike and drink small sips regularly throughout the race. [1] Collect more water form refill stations along the race / from support vehicle. [1] Rehydrate well at the end of each day [1] in preparation for the next stage. [2]

(c) The heart will have to work harder as the blood is more viscous [1] which results in less oxygen supply to the working muscles. [1] Blood flow will be slower as the blood is thicker [1] so less oxygen is supplied to the brain and working muscles, slowing decision making / reaction time / causing cramp. [1] Fewer waste products can be removed from the working muscles [1] as there is reduced blood flow. [1] Lowered blood oxygen levels can cause cramps [1] causing a performer to pull up / retire from activity. [1] [2]

Paper 2, Topic 2

1. A – Having your hips moved over the downhill ski by an instructor. [1]
2. B – Practising a skill repeatedly until it is learned. [1]
3. B – Extrinsic and terminal. [1]
4. (a) Sailing. [1] The environment is constantly changing (wind / current / waves) which the performer needs to make adjustments for. [1] The performer needs to respond to movements by opponent boats in order to outwit them / make counter movements. [1] Movements are performed differently depending on which direction the boat is facing / aiming to go. [1] Answers may vary. [3]
   (b) A – Hitting a forehand from a stationary practice position. [1]
   (c) Accept anywhere in the 'closed' half. [1]

   (d) The skill can be repeated over and over again in the same way [1] to develop muscle memory.[1] The environment in which the skill is applied doesn't change [1] so it can be learned through repetition.[1] Accept other appropriate responses. One mark for knowledge of closed skills/fixed practice. (AO1) One mark for application. (AO2) [2]

5. Complex as it requires making decisions about the type and placement of the ball with several movements involved in the run-up and swing.[1]
Closed as it is performed the same way each time.[1] Accept open as it may depend on the batsman's stance, condition and style.
High organisational skill as it is difficult to break the bowl into different parts.[1] [2]

6. A beginner is unlikely to have developed the strength and muscles associated with golfing [1] so they will need greater breaks in between training sessions to avoid tiredness / fatigue.[1] Beginners may need more motivation than elite performers when they start learning [1] so distributed practice offers a break from the repetitive nature of learning a new skill.[1] Beginners will be new to the skills [1] so they will need time for feedback in between sessions.[1] [2]

7. (a) As a beginner, Jo could be demotivated by unrealistic targets. [1] Jo may be more likely to train if there are specific goals to achieve. [1] Jo may not be motivated to be the best at this stage, just to be the best she can be. [1] Jo needs to focus on her own skills rather than those of others to improve. [1] Goals may help Jo to optimise her performance. [1] Her own performance goals cannot be affected by others, so they are more likely to be achieved by a beginner. [1] [2]
   (b) Measurable – Jo needs to log all her forced and unforced errors in order to calculate her percentage. [1] Achievable – 15% may be too low / difficult to achieve depending on the time frame. [1] Realistic – 15% needs to be achievable given the coaching / practice time available. [1] Time bound – Provide a date by which she must hit the target. [1] [2]
   (c) Achievable goals / goals agreed with a coach / realistic goals [1] are less likely to push performers beyond their maximum causing mental or physical stress. [1] Measurable / realistic goals [a] may provide challenge which motivates performers to use the correct (safe) technique / warm up and cool down properly. [1] [2]
   (d) (i) Visual guidance. [1]
       (ii) Allow error carried forward from part (i).
           Advantages: Quick, concise which is especially good for beginners so they can copy. / Slow motion replays (pausing) can be used for detailed analysis of complex skills. / Can see what to do and form a model of the movement. [1]
           Disadvantages: Complex skills can be difficult to demonstrate clearly. / Performers need to be paying close attention. / Harder to 'feel' the movement or understand the process. [1] [2]

8. Mental rehearsal [1] which involves envisaging the actions of a skill. [1] [2]

9. Intrinsic motivation comes from within the performer, so they can always feel a sense of achievement with progress. [1] Extrinsic factors are likely to be medals in elite championships which can only be won by very few performers. The rest need internal motivation to keep pushing / keep going. [1] Intrinsic motivation may be used as a tool to reach their extrinsic goal, [1] but provides a way to keep putting in continued effort every day. [1] At an elite level, extrinsic factors may be the main motivation left as they have so much time and effort to reach that goal, so intrinsic factors have less importance. [1] [4]

Paper 2, Topic 3

1. D – Running. [1]
2. A – Badminton. [1]
3. This question should be marked in accordance with the levels-based mark scheme provided on **page 123**. [9]

   Indicative content

   AO1 — The potential factors
   Familiarisation with activities available; access; cultural change; subsidies; role models; socio-economic circumstances; role models; stereotyping; media coverage etc.

   AO2 — Application to disabled performers
   Access: as some sports facilities do not cater for the accessibility requirements of all disabilities, access could be improved. Role models: There is a need for more specific disabled role models in the media. Subsidies: Disabled performers could receive subsidies towards transport or membership or access to a sports facility. Stereotyping: There may be a stereotype that disabled users are unable to participate.

   AO3 — Evaluation of the factors
   Ramps for wheelchairs would allow more wheelchair users to access facilities. Targeted campaigns in the media could highlight disabled role models, inspiring others to take part. Those of a low socio-economic circumstance may be able to afford to participate if subsidies for transport and for access are put in place. Promotion and education about disabled sports may help to break stereotypes and start a culture that all people, irrespective of disability can participate.

   Accept any other suitable response that evaluates factors promoting disabled participation.

4. It is summer, so provides a more appealing environment or climate to exercise outdoors in. [1]
5. Two from: disabled [1], over 55s / older people [1], Asian / black / ethnic minority groups [1], lower socio-economic groups / lower income groups [1], minority faith groups [1], single parents.[1] [2]
6. (a) Lower the income, the higher the inactivity or the higher the income the higher the levels of activity. [1]
   (b) Award anywhere in the range 47% and 50% inclusive. [1]
   (c) 53.1 – 45 = 8.1% [1]
   (d) **Promotion:** [1]
   Increase education [1] by advertising the opportunities to get involved in sport / the health benefits / dangers of activity / inactivity. [1] Increase media coverage [1] in local newspapers and magazines of sports and minority groups involved in sports to encourage greater participation. [1] Promote sport in schools for children under 16 [1] to encourage more young people to get into a habit of a healthy lifestyle. [1]

   Provision: [1]
   Provide more facilities at leisure centres / greater access to facilities [1] through subsidised costs / bus services / extended opening hours (outside typical working hours). [1] Provide childcare at gyms or sports clubs [1] in order to provide a solution to parents who otherwise could not take part in activity. [1]

   Access: [1]
   Fund additional programmes for adapted sports [1] to increase accessibility for disabled / less abled people. [1] Create a (discounted) programme of sporting activities for the over 55 year old groups [1] to increase the level of activity in these groups towards that of younger age groups. [1] Introduce / subsidise more women's sports teams / events [1] in order to boost participation by females. [1] [6]

7. (a) Media and broadcasting rights. [1]
   (b) This question should be marked in accordance with the levels-based mark scheme provided on **page 123**. [9]

   AO1 — Knowledge and understanding of the impact of the media on sport
   The media creates more interest in the sport as more people can watch it.
   The sport will earn more money from media coverage and broadcasting rights.
   Media coverage will inform the public about the sport.
   Start times and rules may be dictated by the media to make it more accessible / more enjoyable.

   AO2 — Application of the knowledge of the impact of the media on sport
   Additional money earned from the media can be spent on grass roots sport, larger prize pots, coaching, development, and facilities.
   Media coverage will inform the public about the sport. However, this includes the negatives, causing reputational damage if scandals are publicised in the media, e.g. match fixing.

AO3 — Reasoned judgements about the impact of the media on sport
Greater audiences / broadcast reach means more role models are created which will increase participation in the sport. This can bring in new talent to the sport. However, popularity can make it more expensive to watch which could make it less accessible to those in lower socio-economic groups.
Better or bigger facilities can be built with additional revenues for the public / grass roots teams to use / competitions to be held. However, these would be expensive to operate, and could increase ticket prices / the sport may become too reliant on media income.

The use of data

1. C – The Austrian skier looks uncomfortable at the moment. [1]
2. (a) Correctly labelled x axis (Season/Year) and correctly labelled y axis (Number of yellow cards). [1]
Bars correctly plotted for each season. [1] [2]

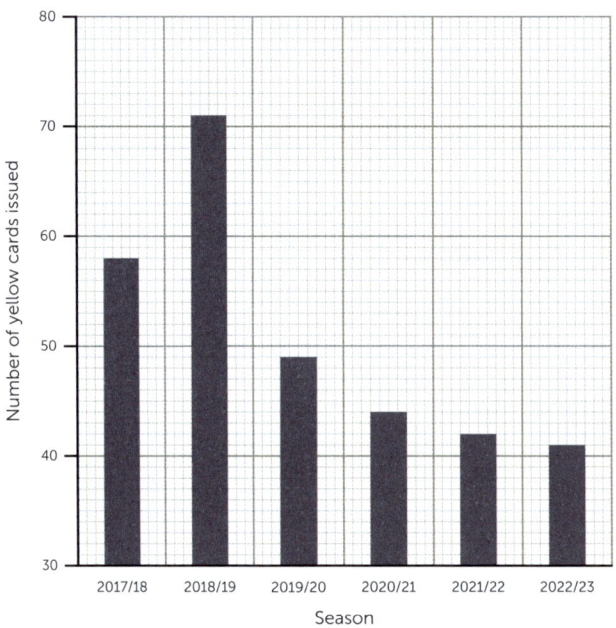

(b) Data for 2018/19 (71) was much higher than other data points and outside of the trend. [1]
(c) Yellow cards generally decreased over the six year period. [1]
(d) Two from: Change of manager with stricter policies on foul play. [1] Change in FA regulations. [1] Club incentives for players to reduce bookings. [1] Change in referee(s). [1] Change in playing style and technique. [1] Greater fitness / ability of players. [1] Greater team bonding and morale. [1] Accept any other reasonable response. [2]
(e) Accept between 38 and 41. [1]

LEVELS-BASED MARK SCHEME FOR EXTENDED RESPONSE QUESTIONS

What are extended response questions?

Extended response questions are worth 6 or 9 marks. These questions are likely to have command words such as 'compare', 'discuss', 'explain' or 'evaluate'. You need to write in continuous **prose** when you answer one of these questions. This means you must write in full sentences (rather than in bullet points), organised into paragraphs if necessary.

You may need to bring together skills, knowledge and understanding from two or more areas of the specification. To gain full marks, your answer needs to be logically organised, with ideas linked to give a sustained line of reasoning.

Example level descriptors

Level descriptors vary, depending on the question being asked. Level 3 is the highest level and Level 1 is the lowest level. No marks are awarded for an answer with no relevant content. The table gives examples of the typical features that examiners are asked to look for in 6 and 9 mark questions.

Level	6 Marks	9 Marks	Descriptors for a method
3	5-6	7–9	• Response contains detailed and accurate knowledge and understanding. Comments are relevant to the context of the question. • Accurate use of technical language and specialist vocabulary. • Responses are always clear, showing correct application of knowledge to the context of the question. Several relevant points, views, or opinions may be presented. • Effective analysis, discussion and development of relevant points, drawing on other relevant areas of the specification. • Comparisons and contrasts may be discussed with a conclusion. • A clear and well-developed line of reasoning has been demonstrated.
2	3-4	4-6	• Response contains mostly accurate knowledge and understanding relating to the question. • Technical language used with some accuracy. • Some responses correctly apply knowledge and reasoning to the context of the question. • Some relevant information referenced in the development of a response but there will be limited analysis of any relevant factors related to the question. • More than one relevant response will have been included supported by a line of reasoning with some structure and an attempt at a conclusion.
1	1–2	1–3	• Basic or isolated knowledge and understanding. • Limited use of or relevance of technical terms. • Responses rarely apply any knowledge to the context of the question. • Little or no reference to other information or attempt to develop a point. • Responses are unstructured and supported by limited evidence.
0	0	0	No answer given or nothing worthy of credit.

NOTES, DOODLES AND EXAM DATES

Doodles

Key dates

Paper 1:
....

Paper 2:
....

COMMAND WORDS

Command word	Definition
Assess	Requires reasoned argument of factors to reach a judgement regarding their importance/relevance to the question context.
Analyse	Break something down into its component parts.
Calculate	Requires computation in relation to fitness data.
Classify	Required to group or place on a scale based on characteristics/analysis of characteristics.
Complete	Required to add information based on a stimulus/resource. This could be to complete a table, graph, chart or missing word/phrase from a sentence/statement.
Define	Required to give the meaning or definition of a word/term.
Describe	Account of something without reasons. Statements in the response need to be linked.
Discuss	Required to explore the issue/situation/problem that is being assessed in the question context, articulating different or contrasting viewpoints.
Examine	Requires a justification/exemplification of a point based on some analysis or evaluation within the response.
Explain	Requires a justification/exemplification of a point. The answer must contain some linked reasoning.
Evaluate	Review/analyse information, bringing it together to form a conclusion/judgement based on strengths/weaknesses, alternatives, relevant data or information. Come to a supported judgement of a subject's qualities and relation to its context.
Give	Generally involves the recall of a fact, or an example based on the given stimulus.
Identify	Can require a selection from a given stimulus or resource.
Justify	Give reasons for answers. This could range from a single response to extended writing answers, depending on question context.
Label	Requires addition of named structures or features to a diagram.
Predict	Often used in data related questions, for example where it requires a prediction of what is likely to happen in future, based on given data.
Select	Requires a choice based on an evaluation of information from a given stimulus/resource.
State	Generally involves the recall of a fact.
Using an example	Often used with explain or describe, where an example is required to exemplify the point(s) being made.
Which	Mainly used in multiple-choice questions where a selection from a set of options is required.

INDEX

0-9
30m sprint test 41

A
abdominal muscles 21
abduction 7
ability 84
adduction 7
aerobic
  endurance 36
  exercise 23
  training zone 44
age 95
agility 36, 39
agonists 11
air 18
alcohol 72
alveoli 20, 52
anabolic steroids 58, 60
anaerobic
  exercise 23
  training zone 44
ankle 4, 6, 7
antagonistic pairs 11
arteries 15, 16
axes of movement 33

B
balance 36
ball and socket joints 6
bar charts 109, 110
basal metabolic rate 71
basic skill 84
beats per minute 26
beta-blockers 58, 60
biceps 10, 11
blood
  cells 2, 16
  clotting 14
  doping 58, 60
  lactate 24
  flow 16, 61
  pooling 61
  pressure 52
  vessels 16
BMI (Body Mass Index) 75
body
  composition 37
  planes 33
  temperature 14
bone 3
  density 51
  marrow 2
bradycardia 52
bronchi 20
bronchioles 20

C
calcium 2, 78
capillaries 16, 52
capillarisation 52
carbohydrate loading 77
carbohydrates 23, 76, 77
carbon dioxide 14
cardiac
  hypertrophy 52
  muscle 9
  output 26, 52
cardio-respiratory system 22, 52
cardiovascular
  endurance 36
  fitness 38, 68
  system 14, 15, 22
carpals 3, 5, 6
cartilage 56
circuit training 47
circumduction 7
clavicle 5
closed skill 84
collar bone 5
commercialisation 99, 100
complex skill 84
components of fitness 36
concurrent feedback 90
concussion 56
condyloid joints 6
continuous training 45
continuum 84
cooling down 61, 63
Cooper 12 minute test 38
coordination 36
cranium 3, 4
culture 97

D
data 108
dehydration 80
deltoid 10
deviance 102
diaphragm 21, 52
diet 71, 76
difficulty continuum 84
diffusion 20, 73
disability 98
discrimination 95, 96, 97, 98
dislocation 56
distributed practice 85
diuretics 58, 60
dorsiflexion 7, 11
double circulatory system 15
drugs 72
  legal recreational 72
  performance enhancing 58
dynamic strength 37
dynamometer test 39

E
education 95
effort 30
elbow 5, 6, 7, 11
emotional health 69, 74
endurance 36, 68
energy balance 79
engagement patterns in sport 95
environmental continuum 84
erythropoietin (EPO) 58
ethnicity 97
excess post-exercise oxygen consumption 22
exercise 24, 35
exhaled air 18
expiration 21
explosive strength 37, 41, 48
extension 7, 11
external obliques 10
extrinsic feedback 90

F

fair play 102
fartlek training 46
fast twitch fibres 12
fat 23, 76, 77
feedback 90
femur 3, 4, 5, 6, 8
fibre 78
fibula 5, 6
fingers 5
first class lever 30, 32
fitness 35
   classes 50
   components 36
   testing 37
   tests 38
FITT 43
fixed practice 85
flat bones 3
flexibility 36, 42
flexion 7, 11
fractures 56
frontal axis 33
frontal plane 33
fulcrum 30

G

gamesmanship 102
gaseous exchange 16, 20, 73
gastrocnemius 10, 11
gender 96
glucose 23
gluteals 10, 11
goal setting 86
golden triangle 99
graphical data 110
grip strength dynamometer 39
growth hormones (GH) 58
guidance 88

H

haemoglobin 20
hamstrings 10, 11
Harvard step test 38
head 4
health 35, 68
heart 15
heart rate 26, 44
high organisational skill 84
hinge joints 6

hip 6, 11
   flexors 10, 11
humerus 3, 4, 5, 6
hydration 78, 80
hypertrophy 51, 77

I

Illinois agility run test 39
imagery 92
inhaled air 18
injuries 56
injury prevention 55
inspiration 21
intercostal muscles 21
interval training 48
intrinsic feedback 90
involuntary muscles 9
iron 78
irregular bones 3

J

joints 2, 6
   synovial 8

K

knee 5, 6, 7, 11
   cap 5

L

lactic acid 14, 22, 23, 24
latissimus dorsi 10
legal recreational drugs 72
leverage 13
levers 2, 30
lifestyle choices 71
ligaments 8, 51
line graphs 109, 111
load 30
long bones 3
longitudinal axis 33
low organisational skill 84
lumen 16
lungs 20

M

macronutrients 77
manual guidance 89
massed practice 85
maximal strength 37

mechanical
   advantage 32
   disadvantage 32
   guidance 89
media 99, 100
   coverage 95, 96, 98
mental preparation 92
mental rehearsal 92
metacarpals 5
metatarsals 4
micronutrients 78
minerals 2, 78
minute ventilation 24
movement 2, 6, 13
movement patterns 33
muscle 10, 61
   fibre types 12
   muscle types 9
muscular endurance 36, 40, 49
musculoskeletal system 13, 51

N

narcotic analgesics 58
nicotine 72

O

obesity 75
one-minute press-up test 40
one-minute sit-up test 40
open skill 84
optimum weight 79
organisational continuum 84
overfat 75
overtraining 43
oxygen 14
oxygen debt 22, 61
oxyhaemoglobin 20

P

PARQ assessment 54
patella 5
pathway of air 20
pathway of the blood 15
pectoralis major 10
pectoral muscles 21
pelvis 3, 4, 6
peptide hormones 58, 60
performance enhancing drugs (PEDs) 58, 102

personal exercise programme (PEP) 70, 115
personal health 70
phalanges 5
physical health 68, 74
pie charts 111
pivot joints 6
planes 33
plantar flexion 7, 11
plasma 17
platelets 2, 14, 17
plyometric training 48
post exercise oxygen consumption (EPOC) 61
posture 13
potassium 78
power 37, 41
practical performance 114
pre-hydration 80
prime mover 11
principles of training 43, 55
progressive overload 43, 55
protection 13
protein 76, 77
  intake 77
  synthesis 77

Q

quadriceps 10, 11
qualitative data 108
quantitative data 108
questionnaires 108

R

radius 5, 6
rate of recovery 52
reaction time 36
red blood cells 17, 52, 59, 73
religion 97
resistance 30
respiratory rate 24
respiratory system 20, 22
rest 51, 57, 71
reversibility 43
ribs 3, 4
RICE 57
role models 96, 97, 98
rotation 7

S

sagittal axis 33
sagittal plane 33
scapula 5, 6
second class lever 31, 32
sedentary lifestyle 74
septum 15
short bones 3
shoulder 5, 6
simple skill 84
sit and reach test 42
skeleton 2, 4, 13
skills 84
slow twitch fibres 12
SMART targets 86
smoking 73
social grouping 95
social health 69, 74
socio-economic group 98
specificity 43
speed 37, 41
spine 4
spirometer trace 19
sponsors 101
sponsorship 99
sport 99
sporting behaviour 102
sportsmanship 102
sprain 56
stamina 38
static strength 37
sternocleidomastoid 21
sternum 3, 4, 5
stimulants 58, 60
strain 56
strength 37, 39, 49
stroke volume 26, 52
surveys 108
synovial joint 8

T

tabular data 109, 110
talus 6
tarsals 3, 4
tendons 8, 51
terminal feedback 90
third class lever 31, 32
tibia 5, 6, 8
tibialis anterior 10, 11
tidal volume 19, 24

toes 5
trachea 20
training
  key principles 43
  thresholds 44
  types 45
  zones 44
transverse axis 33
transverse plane 33
trapezius 10
triceps 10, 11

U

ulna 5, 6

V

valves 15
variable practice 85
vascular shunting 17, 24
vasoconstriction 17
vasodilation 17
veins 15, 16
ventricles 15
verbal guidance 88
vertebrae 3, 4
vertical jump test 41
visual guidance 88
visualisation 92
vital capacity 19, 52
vitamins 78
voluntary muscles 9, 10

W

warming up 61, 62, 92
water 78
weight training 49
white blood cells 17
work:rest ratio 47
wrist 6

Z

zinc 78

EXAMINATION TIPS

When you practice examination questions, work out your approximate grade using the following table. This table has been produced using a rounded average of past examination series for this GCSE. Be aware that boundaries vary by a few percentage points either side of those shown.

Grade	9	8	7	6	5	4	3	2	1	0
Boundary	77%	73%	68%	61%	55%	48%	37%	26%	14%	0%

1. Read each question carefully. This includes any information such as tables, diagrams and graphs.
2. Remember to cross out any work that you do not want to be marked.
3. Answer the question that is there, rather than the one you think is there. In particular, make sure that your answer matches the command word in the question. For example, you need to recall something accurately in a **describe** question but not say why it happens. However, you do need to say why something happens in an **explain** question.
4. Use connective words in your answers, for example, 'because', 'such as', or 'so that' as these force you to give an explanation for your answer, commonly gaining an additional mark in questions worth two or more marks.
5. Ensure that your responses have the appropriate amount of depth based on the number of marks provided and avoid repeating the same point in a variety of ways.
6. Ensure any sporting examples are relevant to the context of the question.
7. In longer answer questions involving levels of response, be sure to include AO1 (knowledge and understanding), AO2 (application of knowledge) and AO3 (analysis and / or evaluation). Give detailed reasons and focus on the impact in AO3. These questions also commonly include knowledge from both sections of the theory specification.
8. Both the examination papers will include multiple-choice questions (MCQs). Make sure you neatly tick the answer you want to be marked. If you change your mind, put a cross in the box (from corner to corner). If you change your mind back again, put a circle neatly around the box.
9. Show all the relevant working out in calculations. If you go wrong somewhere, you may still be awarded some marks if the working out is there. It is also much easier to check your answers if you can see your working out. Remember to give units when asked to do so.
10. Plot the points on graphs accurately and use a ruler. Ensure that you are drawing the type of graph asked for in the questions. Do not confuse bar charts with line graphs. Label all lever diagrams, graphs and charts fully.
11. Write legibly! Candidates often lose marks where examiners are unable to read their handwriting.
12. Write your answers on the lines provided. The lines are usually a good indicator of the length of the expected answer. If you need more space, use additional paper to complete this, clearly numbering the response with the question number. Make it clear that you have used extra paper in the answer space provided.

Good luck!

New titles coming soon!

These guides are everything you need to ace your exams and beam with pride. Each topic is laid out in a beautifully illustrated format that is clear, approachable and as concise and simple as possible.

They have been expertly compiled and edited by subject specialists, highly experienced examiners, industry professionals and a good dollop of scientific research into what makes revision most effective. Past examination questions are essential to good preparation, improving understanding and confidence.

- Hundreds of marks worth of examination style questions
- Answers provided for all questions within the books
- Illustrated topics to improve memory and recall
- Specification references for every topic
- Examination tips and techniques
- Free Python solutions pack (CS Only)

Absolute clarity is the aim.

Explore the series and add to your collection at **www.clearrevise.com**

Available from all good book shops

 @pgonlinepub

ClearRevise — AQA GCSE Food Preparation & Nutrition 8585

ClearRevise — OCR Creative iMedia Levels 1/2 J834 (R093, R094)

ClearRevise — AQA GCSE English Language 8700

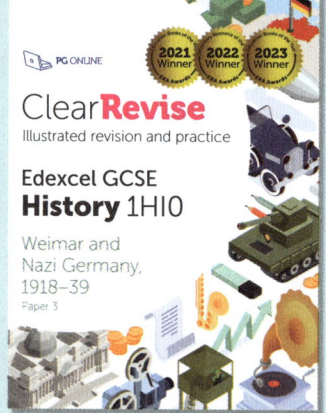

ClearRevise — Edexcel GCSE History 1HI0 — Weimar and Nazi Germany, 1918–39 Paper 3

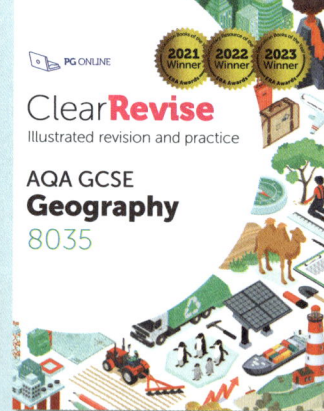

ClearRevise — AQA GCSE Geography 8035

ClearRevise — OCR GCSE Computer Science J277

ClearRevise — AQA GCSE English Literature An Inspector Calls By J. B. Priestley 8702

ClearRevise — Edexcel GCSE Business 1BS0

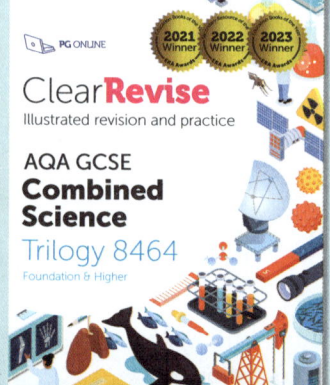

ClearRevise — AQA GCSE Combined Science Trilogy 8464 Foundation & Higher

ClearRevise — AQA GCSE Design and Technology 8552